The Sowing of the Light

KENNETH MACKENZIE

THE PURITAN PRESS

Published by The Puritan Press
353 Great Horton Road
Bradford
West Yorkshire

Cover Design:
Revd. J. V. McKinley

FOREWORD

SINCE MY HUSBAND'S death, in 1983, inquiries have been made as to whether any of his sermons have been published, the implication being that if not they ought to be. Hence this book—a selection from among the many sermons preached over a period of fifty years.

It was his custom to write every sermon down, but because of his remarkable photographic memory he needed neither manuscript nor notes in the pulpit. This resulted in a freedom of delivery much appreciated in the pews. Here the sermons are printed exactly as they were written at the time, and no attempt has been made to update them.

I am hopeful that the printed word, through grace, may do for many future readers what the spoken word did, through grace, for those who, hearing, found their way to God—to whom be the glory. I am very grateful to those of my family and friends who so willingly helped and encouraged me in preparation of the publication, not least to my friend Dr. Skevington Wood for contributing the Preface.

Doris M. Mackenzie.

PREFACE

Dr. Arthur Skevington Wood

OURS is an age which has devalued preaching. Once the glory of the Church, it is nowadays regarded by many as irrelevant and unnecessary. Where it does not meet with stony indifference its reception is often blatantly hostile. As Professor Klaas Runia argues in a recent book, the sermon is under attack from outside the Church and, more sadly, even from within. The mood of the times is generally inimical to the pulpit.

Despite these unfavourable climatic conditions preaching still continues. Indeed it is a divinely ordained and a divinely honoured means of communication. The effective proclamation of the written Word brings about an encounter with Christ the living Word and nothing in life can be more significant than that. This was the hallmark of Kenneth Mackenzie's preaching, as the sermons in this selection will show. He was above all a servant of the Word — seeking always, however, to relate it to the human situation. His congregations could hardly fail to be stirred.

It was said that, before the impact of the Evangelical Revival was felt, eighteenth century sermons could be divided into three categories: dull, duller, and dullest. Mackenzie's preaching was at the farthest possible remove from dullness. Both in content and in presentation it was calculated to stab the spirits of the hearers broad awake, if we may adapt a phrase of Robert Louis Stevenson. This is preaching at its highest and best: as such it provides impressive evidence that it is by no means obsolete.

It was my privilege not only to hear Kenneth Mackenzie on occasion but also to know him as a friend. We shared a mutual concern to preserve and declare the truth of the Gospel. He preceded me as a minister in the York Wesley Circuit, as it then was, and I reaped the benefit of his tireless labours. I am delighted to find that his printed messages still convey the fire and force of the original. My prayer is that they may not only lead us to thank God for such a fearless and indeed prophetic ministry but also enable us to "grow in the grace and knowledge of our Lord and Saviour Jesus Christ." (2 Peter 3 : 18).

CONTENTS

POSSESSING OUR POSSESSIONS

Obadiah v. 17: The House of Jacob shall possess their possessions.

HOW is that? *Shall* possess their possessions? Surely, if a man possess a thing, he possesses it now. How is it possible to say: "These are that man's possessions. He does not possess them now, but the day will come when he will. He will possess his possessions"?

And yet . . . and yet. Take this man, a peasant farmer in the Third World. He owns a bit of land. It costs him much labour and gives him starvation rations. The yield per acre is poor. There does not seem to be much nutriment in the soil, and then it happens that, when the feeble crop is growing green, the greenness goes for want of water, the drought persists and the crops wither.

Then, on a day, along comes a man who takes a handful of soil here and a handful there, and returns to tell him that his soil lacks a certain chemical, and how he may get it. Then he tells him that deeper than his primitive ploughshare there is richness in the soil, and a machine will be coming that will bite deep and turn it up. And the machine will plough the whole farm in a day. And this official now wants permission to drill for water. And so he drills, and on a day when the dry land is cracked, there is a sudden gush of water. The nutriment in the soil and the underground lake were always his, but now he possesses his possessions.

One example is enough to set the mind darting here and there, snatching up instances of possessions not yet possessed . . . and yet again of men beginning to possess their possessions. I suppose as children of the human race our possessions in the fields of knowledge and art are so immense that we can never hope to lay our hands upon them all. Thus the Greek poetry of Homer is as much mine as anybody's. It is free to me. I may not have entered into possession; I may never enter into possession, but in a certain sense it is mine; it is there for me to take up. The discovery of penicillin has been one of the great events of our century. But, mark this, the penicillin in itself was not a new creation. Penicillin had been in the world for endless ages. And, in the sense that man had been given dominion over the earth, penicillin had long been our possession, but only recently have we possessed our possession.

The romance of the missing heir has figured in many a tale, but often it has been real enough. Days were when our far-flung empire beckoned to the adventurous, to the wasters, and to those who had made the home-country too hot to hold them. Many of them were lost to sight. Sometimes it happened that an unexpected estate fell to one of them. Then the search. Advertisements in dominion, colonial and American papers. Here was a man, who had great possessions, but had not yet possessed his possessions.

Now I do not know if any solicitor had the experience of explaining to the unkempt and shabby man on the other side of his desk, that he was heir to a considerable fortune, listing the estates, the balances in banks, the stocks and shares, and then for the other to ask if he could spare a couple of bob for a cup of tea. Then for the man of law to explain again in simple words, but as impressively as he could, and then for the other to ask if he could go now, else he might be too late to book a bed in the Salvation Army Hostel.

But I know this. I have had, and not once only, and not twice only, I have had one before me hagridden by guilt, *by guilt,* broken in mind, and I have sought to explain and enforce the meaning of the Cross of Christ, of a great redemption that was wrought, and a great Atonement that was made, but my words have been like pebbles rattling against a stone wall. One woman there was in middle-life, and I took her through the great Scriptures one by one, and then I said: "Come now with me to the Church, and we shall have the service of Holy Communion, and you will have the bread and the wine, tokens to you of a complete forgiveness that is offered." But she would not come. "No," she said, "it is too late for me."

Too late? But I read that One died for all, that Christ died for our sins according to the Scriptures, that Christ died for the ungodly, that on a certain day, at Passover-time, when Pontius Pilate was procurator of Judea, Jesus Christ was set forth to be a propitiation for our sins, and not for our sins only but for the sins of the whole world, meaning that on that day a reckoning was made of all sins committed by all men in every place since the dawn of time, and of the sins yet to be committed to the end of time, and the price, the incredible price, was paid, and thus the offer of forgiveness is nigh thee, in thy heart and in thy mouth, pushed up to your very finger-tips. It's yours, and you have but to possess your possessions.

There's a big Mission Hall in Rochdale, Champness Hall. Thomas Champness did a remarkable work there in his day. Well, at one time he was a missionary in West Africa. In the place where he worked there was a rich native woman of a large heart who used to buy slave babies and care for them well. She belonged to the Christian mission. So did her son. When she died he inherited her slaves. One of them, a girl, fell in love with a young fellow that went to the mission, and with the permission of the slavemaster, she married her William, and they had several children. Now the ugly part. The slave-master renounced his Christianity and became an idolator again. He became bitter against the mission. To do it an injury he announced his intention of selling William's wife, the slave girl, and her children, into different parts of the country. Now Champness stepped in. He wrote home for money and sent to the slave-master and offered to buy the woman and her children. The fellow required an extortionate price. So Champness took the matter to the native Court. The Court ordered the fellow to sell the woman and the children to Champness, and stipulated the market price.

So Champness went to the woman and told her. What did she do? Burst into tears, gather her brood and make her way back to the slave master? Not she! Champness said: "She clapped her hands, she sang and she danced!" Her freedom had been bought with a price, and she possessed her possession.

And it would be wrong for any here to leave this church to-day still to carry a burden of guilt, for your forgiveness has been bought with a price. It is yours. Possess your possessions.

Perhaps the realm of human experience where it is most apposite to speak of possessing our possessions is the realm of power. And, in the onward march, man has recognised more and more sources of power, and has increasingly possessed his possessions. Some primitive warrior discovered that the springiness in a bent branch could hurl his spear much farther than a simple throw. So the bow and arrow came into use. He learned to employ the power in the muscles of the horse, the dog, the ox, the camel and the elephant, then the power exerted by the wheel and the lever. It was a major step forward when he first harnessed the wind to drive his simple boat and later the power of the mill-stream to grind his corn. Then were introduced fire and the steam engine, then the internal combustion engine, the conversion of heat into electrical power . . . And now the threatened famine of power, and we are beginning to reckon up what possessions of power we have that we might possess our possessions, learning how to harness the heat of the sun, the power in the tide, in the rolling wave, and always marching alongside us now, the promise and the threat of nuclear fission. There you have a vivid elucidation of our principle. The power in the atom is nothing new. The power was there in the first moment of Creation. And when man came, and insofar as he had the overlordship of nature, the power in the atom was his possession, but he had to wait until this century before he possessed his possession.

But besides that naked physical power, there are powers of other kinds. There is psycho-physical energy, deployed in the muscle and deployed in the brain, energy consumed in hard labour, and in hard thinking. It has attracted half a dozen names—nurin, neurokyme, elan vital. Here again there is ample evidence that we have a greater reservoir of this power than most of us imagine. Even in the course of a fairly energetic life we only employ a part of what we possess, and so continue until the clap and stroke of dire emergency, and then the hidden energy begins to flow and we possess our possessions. I wish there were time to display the evidence, but we must come to that which concerns us most—spiritual power.

I recall, from a long time ago, a Laymen's Missionary Conference at Swanwick. I remember an Australian, a medical doctor, a character of quaint and forceful speech. He said that he had been in conversation with his grocer, down under. This grocer, knowing well that the doctor was a pillar of the local church, said that if he ran his grocer's business as they ran their church he would be bankrupt. How so? Well, in his business he had to use all his assets. "But what assets don't we use?" "Do you mean the Bible?" "No." "Prayer?" "No." "Preaching?" "No." "What then?" "God! You don't use God." Interesting grocers they have in Australia.

We don't use God.

Well, of course, we all know that the Scriptures are thick with promises of power, of grace, of the strength of the Presence of Divine might, and of how all this illimitable resource is freely offered. We have only to ask, to reach out, to open our hands, and it is ours, ours as the children of God, ours as the company of the redeemed. Not ours simply to flaunt and flourish, but ours to use, to deploy, for by the very nature of the task we are given, we need Divine power—to redeem the fallen race, to redeem fallen nature, to clear the mountains of sin out of the way, to reverse the horrid work of centuries, to pluck the taint out of the blood, to break the kingdoms of this world with a rod of iron and to keep on doing it while the generations rise and fall. For this we need Divine Power. O, we need to possess our possessions!

Do you remember Mount Carmel, and the burnt mountainside and the pitiless sun riding above, and the drama in the making? Elijah, the prophet of God and, pitched over against him, Ahab and Jezebel, and all the court of the king and all the martial power, and that other power, the priests of Baal. And there was to be a contest, not with weapons of iron and brass, but a contest of the spirit. Two altars. On each a sacrifice. An altar for Baal, an altar for the Lord, and the four hundred and fifty priests of Baal were to pray to their gods to send down fire, and Elijah would pray to his Lord to send down fire. And the God that answereth by fire, let him be God.

Now forget about Elijah and watch the priests of Baal. See them move out, four hundred and fifty of them, each in his tunic, with the sign of the Baalim woven upon the breast, dignified and decorous they come, and they begin to chant their prayers. Now they gyrate about the altar, and from time to time they fling up their arms, and their incantations become louder. So they prayed until noon, and then the excitement seized them. They broke rank, and began to leap on and off the altar. These men were now in agony of supplication, screaming into the sky, mouthing the devil names of the Baalim. Standing over against them was Elijah and they could hear the biting, mocking things he said. And now it began to get rough. Tunics were torn off. Each priest drew from the scabbard his sacrificial knife, honed to a razor edge and the slashing began. They cut themselves in the frenzy, and you might see the blood mingled with the sweat shining in the sun, and dabbling the track they took. The shadows were lengthening now, but still they called and still they cried, as if they would bring down the very gods by the fervour of their praying.

I say, if there had been anything that could come, it would have come that day; if there had been only a guttering candle-flame, they would have drawn it down by the importunity of their praying, and possession to be possessed they would have possessed it.

So they live in history, the heathen priests, as a rebuke to Christian men, Christian men who deploy but feeble resources, not because they are without, but because they will not bestir themselves to possess their possessions.

But there is the promise. It has been fulfilled before, and it will be fulfilled again, the House of Jacob shall posssess their possessions.

For the third and final point I have to remind myself that I speak to a people with great expectations. There is always an element of the precarious about our earthly expectations. Half a dozen things could go wrong. One might even die before one's inheritance arrives. But there is nothing precarious about the expectations of which I speak. For you are heirs of God, and joint heirs with Christ; for you there is an inheritance incorruptible and undefiled. Yes, the riches of the glory of His inheritance in the saints.

You stand heir to the great estate. It is sometimes called the Father's House; sometimes, the City that hath Foundations, whose Builder and Maker is God; or the Better Country; or, the "place prepared for you," the Scots call it "the lang hame," and I have heard it called the upper rose garden; sometimes, simply, heaven.

With any earthly estate, at the best you have it for a short time and then leave it behind, but your spiritual inheritance fadeth not away. Holding your earthly estate, you could lose what you have through civil commotion or national convulsion, but this inheritance that fadeth not away is reserved in heaven for you.

An Estate or Land Agent could give you a fair description of a property that is hither and now, but no detailed description of your eternal inheritance is available. It seems that it is above our language and beyond our dreams.

Now this is your possession, but you have not yet possessed it?

There is, however, a possession which you may possess now, and indeed, *do* possess, and that is the earnest of your inheritance. (Eph. 1:14). Linger with me a moment about this word "earnest." There is an equivalent word which you will not find in most dictionaries—the word "arles"——ARLES. Perhaps you have never heard that word. I did not know it until I came to venerable years. Now you would not think that the word "earnest" and the word "arles" come from the same root, but they do. They can be tracked back through middle English and Gaelic and Old French to the Latin *arrhae, arrabon* (Gk), *eravon* (Heb.), brought by Phoenicians into Italy and Greece.

The Greek *arrabon* once meant an engagement ring. It was a pledge. So with the old "arles-penny," or "erres-penny" or "earnest penny." It was a pledge penny given in a transaction, a promise of more to come of the same kind.

So with an arles. It was once part of the legal system. A man negotiated to buy an estate. A bargain was struck. There was, however, much yet to do in the way of documents, etc. But a spadeful of earth was lifted, bagged and carried away by the purchaser. Or, if there was a field of corn, several ears would be plucked and given to the purchaser, and such things were legal pledges, some little part of the same stuff and substance as the estate he was to have.

This is the word . . . *arrabon* . . . an earnest in Eph. 1:14, an earnest of our inheritance—to be had now, to be *held* now, to be *possessed* now. And so you may do, for there are times when the peace of God descends upon your soul and it seems as if heart and mind sail on a calm pool of tranquillity, and you feel very close to God. This is the earnest of your inheritance.

Or you stumble on a situation, and there is the plight of a person, or it may be an animal, or so small a thing as a bird with a broken wing, and you could cry, and you are moved by loving-kindness and your heart melts towards this other, this person, this tiny creature. That, too, is the earnest, for loving-kindness reigns supreme in the inheritance yet to be.

And what other things? Perhaps a few moments of ecstatic joy, taste it and let it go, and thank God for the sign, the earnest, the arles, the pledge of the inheritance reserved in heaven for you.

Thus now we may possess the pledge, the foretaste, the forward-thrown experience of that which is to be. And after that the House of Jacob shall possess their possessions. O it shall! There may be some dark roads to travel before we come to it; there will be some pains to endure and some tears to weep, but we shall therein and thereat take tight hold of our earnest, our pledge, our *arrabon* until all journeys overpast, and we shall forever possess our eternal possessions.

THE DIVINE BORROWER

Luke 19:31: And if any one ask you, Why do ye loose him? thus shall ye say, The Lord hath need of him.

BEGINNING with this text, there are two different trails one might follow. One asks the question why, in a book so economical of words, they should give space to the mere mechanics of hiring an animal, even the animal on which the Lord Jesus was to ride into Jerusalem. Then one senses something conspiratorial in the text, as of secret dealings; the same thing is in the arrangements for the Last Supper. That is one trail to follow.

The other trail begins with the simple contemplation of the words, "The Lord hath need of him," and the sudden sense that here in a sentence we have the whole story of Christian dedication, of treasure poured out, of labour undergone, and of blood spilt.

Jesus borrowed a colt. It was natural enough. He had no beast of His own, and He needed one. It was not by any means the only thing He borrowed. In fact from the beginning to the end of the days of His flesh, He seemed always to be borrowing. And in that we hear the warning note we find elsewhere in the Gospel, we see the upheld cautioning hand, the red glow of the danger signal.

He borrowed somebody's stable in which to be born: He borrowed an animal's manger for a cradle; and after the hidden years, when He came forth into the ministry, He was always borrowing. You will remember that incident when His enemies tried to trap Him into treasonable talk, and raised the question of paying tribute to Caesar. He answered them adroitly, but needed a coin for the lesson, and said, "Shew Me the tribute money." Then they brought him a penny. The natural thing for any other man would have been to feel for a coin in his own money-belt, but apparently He did not have a penny. He borrowed one.

He said, "The foxes have holes, and the birds of the air have nests, but the Son of Man hath not where to lay His head." No house. No home. So when He slept in a bed, it was a bed He had borrowed. And when He was under a humble roof, and there was no bed to spare, He would sleep on the floor, and the floor-space was borrowed. You remember how He borrowed a fishing-boat for a pulpit, and how He borrowed five loaves and two fishes from a small boy to feed the multitude. He borrowed other people's children to caress and fondle—He had none of His own. So He borrowed this colt for the triumph-ride into Jerusalem, and He borrowed an upper-room for the Last Supper. When He staggered under the load on the Via Dolorosa, He borrowed the strength of Simon of Cyrene to carry His Cross. On the Cross He borrowed from John, care, comfort and shelter for His stricken mother. He begged some sour wine from a soldier there that He might clear His throat for that mighty triumphant cry, "Tetelestai!" "It is accomplished!" And when He was dead He borrowed another man's tomb to rest His body for a space. Jesus Christ, the Divine Borrower!

And as He was in the days of His flesh, so He is in the eternal years of His Spirit. He borrows still. Come ye within reaching distance of Jesus Christ, and you will find His hand stretched out for something. For the curious thing is that this King of Kings, this Lord of Lords, has nothing at all resembling what we commonly count as our possessions. He has no car, but you and I can think of a hundred purposes for which He might want a car. So He has to borrow one, and a driver for it. And your memory will tell you of many occasions when He has borrowed you and your car. I might begin there with an endless catalogue, but a small selection will suffice. Once on a weekday I went into the Sunday School, and found there an oldish man, a retired carpenter. He looked a bit abashed as he explained he had noticed some of the Sunday School chairs were unserviceable, and he had just slipped in to see if he could straighten them out. So Christ the Divine Carpenter, will borrow a man's skill and labour. Then at the Overseas Mission Sale of Work, you will see a table laden with pots of home-made jam. Somebody has been busy in a steaming kitchen. Good. Christ can use the jam. I knew of a farmer's wife one of whose chores was raising the poultry. She always reckoned to raise a couple of ducks for the missionary fund. If any of her ducks died, by some mysterious changes of identity, they were never the missionary ducks. Small things and simple things? Yes, but it could be that He wants a hospital in some place where they've never heard of a hospital, and then there is a massive corporate borrowing. But He has His way, and there in time is the hospital to prove it. And so endlessly on, Christ reaches out His insatiable hands, ships and aircraft and each with a heavy load, tractors and water-pumps and Bibles by the million. The Lord hath need of them. It makes Christianity an expensive religion. A man's hand is never out of his pocket.

One hears the querulous complaint from time to time: "If it isn't one thing it's another; it's for the needy young, or the needy old; it's for the lepers or the spastics. If it's not for something near at hand, it's for something at the ends of the earth. Straight appeals, and tickets for a coffee morning, and what with rates and taxes, and inflation it's getting a little much."

Blame Christ! He may hold the whole world in His hand, but He holds out the other hand empty, and as often as it is filled it comes back empty. Expensive religion it is, but when you come to think of it, you would despise it if it weren't.

But of course this is only part of the story. Christ borrows men and women. "Come ye after Me," He would say. "Come, follow Me." He had in mind for those He called an incredible destiny. They were to be children in the Father's house beyond the dust and shadows of this world, but on the way they would know beatings, persecutions and violent death. Christ did not mince words. For the most part the evangelical appeals and persuasions of our modern day set out the blessings and the glories of the Christian life, and this is well, but not so often does the sternness appear, the perils that lie in wait, the fierce cost that may be required.

To Peter and Andrew Christ said, "Come ye after Me, and I will make you to become fishers of men." The story has it that Peter was crucified in Rome, head downwards; and that Andrew was crucified in Patros, not nailed but bound with ropes, it was reckoned a severer punishment because it took longer to die. He called to Matthew, counting coins there at the tax-gatherer's table, "Come, follow Me." They say he died in India, where he had gone to preach the Gospel, the blade of a spear in his heart. Mark they caught in Alexandria, tied him by the heels to the back of a chariot, and dragged him through the streets. They threw his battered frame into a prison, and the next day burned him. James the brother of John died by Herod's sword.

Jesus stopped Paul on the Damascus Road, and borrowed him. He did not ask if he had other plans. He explained at the time . . . "For he is a chosen vessel unto Me to bear My name before the Gentiles and Kings, and the children of Israel; for I will shew him how great things he must suffer for My name's sake." And shew him He did. How did Jowett say? He once saw the track of a bleeding hare across the snow. That was the track of the Apostle Paul across Europe. The Lord had need of him.

You remember that almost the last words He said to His disciples, and through them to us all, when He was received up into the cloud! "Ye shall be My witnesses." It is a grim fact that the Greek word we so translate is *martures.* Witnesses and martyrs, martyrs and witnesses.

I have read that in the years that followed there was a School of Witnesses in a secret place in Italy. There Christians went for a course. Part of the course was physical. They trained hard, reckoning that a fit body could better endure pain than soft flesh. They denied themselves of food to the point of ravening hunger, and of drink to the point of raging thirst, reckoning that they would not be so easily thrown by those enemies if they had looked into their faces already. The book-work was to read and get by heart the things the great martyrs had said in their last and tested moments, so that they might say something of the kind when their turn came. Above all, they repeated many times a day, when they rose, and when they laid themselves down . . . "Christianus sum." "I am a Christian. I am a Christian." So that if they could say nought else, they might say that through their clenched teeth.

But you know how through their witness the Word spread like fire. The Lord had need of them.

It would be wrong to be unbalanced here. The Church

has had her times of rest. Many a Christian has lived his life through without the threat of steel or fire. When the Gospel wins its way, it changes not only lives but societies, and the day surely comes when the Christian is not hunted but honoured, when the Holy Spirit asserts His mastery in whole villages, when something new and cleansing and transforming spreads through a countryside. I can take you to places now where you can go through a gate into the next farm, and then over a stile into the next, then cross a bit of a road and stand on the soil of the next, and so on and on, and you have been on six or seven farms, and there is a Christian family in every farmhouse. The Lord hath need of them. But no blood is spilt, and no man is struck in the face because he belongs to Christ.

Of course we never know when hell will erupt again, or where. Our own century has its noble army of martyrs, and the ranks fill up year by year.

Now here is the stabbing question: Why do they put up with it? With this hand always reaching out for what they've got? With this imperious tap on the shoulder, almost as if they are under arrest? And having been ensnared in the first place, why do they stick it out? Take but one instance—that School for Witness—the training school for brutal death. They did not arrive there a band of jaunty youngsters, starry-eyed with romantic hopes. They came grim-faced through the dark by secret ways. But by what mystery did they come, and by what mystery did they stay?

Perhaps the secret can be traced by means of the things that Jesus borrowed, as if He left upon each such borrowed thing, something of Himself, something that I can only think of as a gleam of glory. So He borrowed a stable to be born in. There's not really much to a stable.

Serviceable, yes, but you don't go in in your best clothes. Commonplace. But there is one stable towards which the eyes of half the world turn at least once a year. Kings and the great ones of the earth have knelt there, and the unnumbered poor, footsore from the pilgrimage, poorer by their life-savings, eyes moist with a holy joy. He was born there and He left His glory upon it.

It may be known among you that there was at Rome in that day a plinth called the Lactarian column. Unwanted babies were left at the foot of it. The slave-dealers used to pick them over, the sturdiest were taken and kept in the compounds and fed on the swill until they were old enough for the market. Magicians would take some of them to use the brain-matter for making magic potions. In other places an unwanted child would be put into a jar and floated out of sight down the river. In others they would be put out naked on a frosty night. But there in Judea was One who said, "Suffer the little children to come unto Me and forbid them not," and He took them in His arms and blessed them. And thereafter where His Gospel went, there went the children's charter and a glory rested on their heads.

We thought of how Jesus borrowed a man's strength to carry His Cross. There are many nameless ones in the Gospels, but this man's is given, and not only his name, but where he came from, and added to that the names of his two sons. Simon of Cyrene, the father of Alexander and Rufus, was the man. How arresting that is! Those for whom Mark initially wrote must have known Alexander and Rufus, and they must have known them because their names were current in the early Church. We speculate, O yes, we speculate, but I see it thus, Alexander and Rufus were Christ's men because Simon their father was Christ's man, and he became Christ's man on that dreadful uphill road to Calvary. When the soldiers discharged him, he took with him more than an aching back. What passed between him and our blessed Lord we do not know, but he was touched with the glory.

And then the tomb, Joseph of Arimathea's tomb that He borrowed to rest His body for a night and a day and a night. Little did Joseph think in an earlier day as he watched the workman hewing that tomb out of the rock, that one day that tomb, empty and open, would be the sign to untold millions that death had been trodden down by the Divine Victor, and the Kingdom of Heaven flung wide open to all believers. Grim and terrible was the borrowing of that tomb, but the ineffable glory was bestowed upon it!

But more than all this, He touches with glory those men and women who are taken into His borrowing hand.

He borrowed the person of Levi, otherwise Matthew. Now he was a publican, a tax-gatherer for Rome, an outcast from his own people, numbered with the riff-raff. Men like that are on the downward slope. But Jesus reached out a hand for him. Years later, this same man, with the face of a visionary, was on his way to India, to preach this same Jesus who takes broken men and makes them whole, a rough road and a perilous, and ending in violent death. But will you count the times and the places where a voice has been heard saying, "Our lesson is taken from the Gospel according to St. Matthew," or the times and the places where a man, in his secret place, hungry for life, has turned the pages of the Gospel according to St. Matthew? What glory to bestow upon a man! Paul has a phrase, "an eternal weight of glory." He must have known that he was outraging language when that phrase was torn out of him. But he speaks of the unspeakable.

To Paul we turn, for if any man knew the cost, he

did, and if any man knew the glory, he did. "He is a chosen vessel unto Me," said Jesus, when He borrowed him. "I will shew him how great things he must suffer for My sake." And we want to know how such men stick it out. Nay, we want to know more than that; how they sing their way through it. Nay, more even than that, how they seem to welcome the whips and the stones with positive enjoyment.

There is a vivid picture in Acts 16 to which I can never turn without bewilderment. The time is midnight. The place, the jail in Philippi—and that jail, the achaeologists tell us, was built over a sewer; the place would stink. The characters are Paul and Silas, and each in a sorry state. Earlier that day they had been flogged with leaded rods—historians tell us that criminals often died under the rods—and then their rags had been thrown round their torn backs, and they had been dragged to the jail. There their feet had been made fast in the stocks. Ponder that. Exhausted, they would crave sleep, if the pain would allow. But they must sleep face down for their backs were stiff with wounds and caked blood. But how do you sleep face down when your feet are fast in the stocks? Hear then the testimony of Scripture, "But about about midnight Paul and Silas prayed and sang praises unto God." The prayers I can take in. In like state, you and I would pray; broken prayers, prayers like cries, prayers mingled with groans. But "sang praise!" Picking out some lilting psalm, one of them pitching the note; perhaps one a tenor and the other a baritone; then letting it go. Let it go they did, for the prisoners heard them. When you know the secret of that midnight singing, you know the secret of the persecuted who stick it out, of the serenity of those about to die. Ask Paul, and he will tell you, "Most gladly therefore will I rather glory in my weaknesses, that the power of Christ may rest upon me." "When I am weak, then am I strong."

Standing outside it all, it is plain to any observer, that Paul had some inner resource, and that inner resource was a potent thing, no sudden rush of euphoria, but a persistent, undying power that bestowed upon this hunted, wounded, battered man an invincibility, equal in its defence against troubles of many kinds, and appearing, not in some grim stoical form, but to bestow a lyrical, smiling, rejoicing spirit upon this man. That is crystal clear. But such a power, such a glory, belongs to that catalogue of things that cannot be known unless they be experienced. What is also clear is that Paul was not alone. Something new had come into the world at Pentecost, and there we see the head of that procession which was to lengthen and widen with every generation. The mystery men and the mystery women of history. Frail flesh carrying the glory of divine power. If a young man were to set himself to read every account and record of these witnesses, his life span would be gone before he had finished.

Must it not be so? Would the Jesus Christ whose face you see in the Gospels take up a man into His service, lay upon him burdens of suffering, and leave him to go it alone? And something more, would this divine enterprise ever have been begun, with all its cost to God and to men, if the end to be achieved had not been worth all that went before? Paul has it that the sufferings of this present time are not worthy to be compared with the glory that shall be revealed. What a glory that must be! What heights of rapture! What incredible bliss! Let Emmanuel show His five wounds received on Calvary, let the saints show their scars, let the missionaries trace out their long journeys, and speak of martyrdoms far from home. And all that is not to be compared with the glory which shall then be revealed.

Preachers, take note! Taking your text, you have always known that it was a time of high drama. One factor in that drama was the possibility that someone who heard, might, from that hour, strike out in a new direction, and that the new direction might be fraught with danger. A minister I knew returned after a lapse of years to a place where he had served. He met a close acquaintance of those days who recalled to his mind an occasion when he had preached one Sunday afternoon at a Girl Guides' Rally. Did the minister remember what he preached about? He shook his head. Evidently he had preached about the Holy Spirit and had urged the girls to hand over the direction of their lives to Him. One girl did. She was now a missionary in Central Africa. The minister felt humbly grateful that he had been used, but confessed to a sense of something like dismay. Central Africa, he felt, was no place for a girl.

The weight that rests upon the preacher is fearful, but if he is ready to sink under the load, he is to remember that there is no price Christ asks him to pay, and no price his hearer is asked to pay, but Christ holds His shield over that man's head, and He brings him to the glory not to be expressed, the joy unspeakable.

THE PARABLE OF THE MIRRORS

2 Cor. 3 : 18 : But we all with open face, beholding as in a mirror, the glory of the Lord, are changed by that same image from glory to glory, even as by the Spirit of the Lord.

IF SOMEONE should have come into this place looking for a change, this text will be his guidepost. All the more if he says . . . the cry in my bones, the ache in my heart is for a change in me . . . not a change of air, not a change of house, or a change of job . . . It is not for a change of government or of economic policy. I have grown out of all that. The cry in my bones is for a change in me: I am the man who inflicts my deepest wounds. I am the source of my sorrows: I am the destroyer of my dreams. I want a change, and I want the change in me. If there is such a man, this is the word that speaks to you.

Katop-triz-omenoi. I can scarely lay my tongue to it. Greek word, of course, embedded in the original text, and hard to translate . . . you will find the several versions have slightly different translations here.

The word has to do with mirrors, but is so constructed as to imply that we are mirrors. So to the Parable of Mirrors . . . and to the likeness between the mirror of glass and the human mirrors, and after that the several and instructive differences.

First, the glass takes into its heart what it looks at. So does the human mirror— take into its heart what it looks at, and that is the simple, but life-and-death truth, expounded in this Scripture.

But as there is a likeness, so there are differences.

The first is this, the common mirror is a *simple device,* a plate of transparent glass, silvered as to one side.

But the human mirror is *anything but simple,* for we are fearfully and wonderfully made. It has several receptors . . . Waves of light fall on the retina of the eye; sound waves vibrate within the ear; smells stimulate the nerve endings in the nose, flavours titillate the taste-buds of the mouth. Temperature, touch and pain each arouse special nerve endings on the skin, and stir up receptor nerves in the interior of the body. So code messages race along the nerve-fibres to the brain. Now the high mystery . . . the brain breaks down the code, and flashes images onto the screen of the mind.

With the looking glass then, a process comparatively simple, but with the human mirror, one fearfully intricate . . . but both the same in this, they take into their hearts what they look at.

Now a second difference. The glass will take into its heart a pebble or the crown jewels with equal precision, and with equal *indifference.* It will take in the table laid for the great feast, the crystal, the gleaming silver, the white napery, or it will take in the pig-swill in the trough, and each with equal indifference.

But the human mirror brings to what it sees differences of interest and intensity.

Out for a spin on a fine day, the driver will have a kaleidoscope of unfolding beauty haunting the corner of his eye . . . but he must keep his eye on the road, be deaf to the coos and cries of his passengers. But they arrive at the picnic spot, and the car is parked. And now his slow, contemplative eye takes it all in. The gaze travels slowly from close at hand to the far horizon; wanders slowly down the present hill, rests upon the river, then upon the herd in the meadow; climbs the opposite rise, holds for a moment to follow the shadow of a cloud across it, climbs to the high peaks, slowly swinging from one to the next. Someone says, "Have a sandwich," but he does not hear, The old fashioned Biblical word for that is *beholding.*

I do not mean that what we glance at is lost to the mind, but only that when we behold, we take a firmer grip.

The student knows it. It is one thing to let your eye run down the page of a book, with your feet up, breaking off now and then for a bit of conversation . . . and quite another thing to sit at your desk with a heavy tome, taking notes, now reaching for a dictionary or the encyclopaedia, scratching your head, turning back a page, to get another grip of the slippery argument. That is beholding.

A third difference. When the ordinary mirror is turned in a new direction, *it loses at once the image it first held in its heart.* Turn it towards a sunset, and then turn it towards the wall of a house. It is now as if it never saw a sunset at all.

Not so the *human mirror.* Whatever it takes into its heart *it keeps.* Always the gaze is swivelling this way and that. Every day processions of pictures march through the mind. You may see a thing but once, and see it no more, but it is yours for ever. I once saw volcanic smoke spurting out of Mount Etna. Once I saw it, and did not pass that way again, but in my mind's eye, I can see it now. The neurologist tells us that each of us has more brain cells than the number of people on earth. They speak of memory traces etched on the brain cells, as if it were a vast computer bank, storing away the images as they come. But we have always known the broad truth, simply because we remember things, nursery rhymes and multiplication tables, faces and scenes of long ago, things said, and music played. If all the things any one of us could remember were set down in books, we should need a large library to contain the volumes.

But something more, and this of vast importance. The things we can recall are only a part of what is in the store. Do we not, in our dreams, have images of things we have not thought of for many years? Or meet a childhood friend; he relates an incident of long ago . . . Something dawns and we say: "Bless me! it's all coming back now." And then the psychologist tells us there is much more. He has devices for driving deep shafts into the mines of the memory . . . hypnotism, word association and the like, so that it is fairly surmised that we lose nothing of all we have received.

There is yet one more difference. There is *no permanent effect* upon the glass mirror from what it looks at. It can hang for forty years opposite a Rembrandt, or opposite a picture window that looks out on a scene where the meadows and the woods run down to where the waves are creaming over the yellow sand and the brown rocks. But take the mirror down and no trace of beauty lingers with it. Face it with a dead rat on a dunghill, and then turn it away, and no smudge of ugliness is left to stain the mirror.

Not so the human mirror. *There is never a moment when we are not subject to the forces of change.* The man who comes home from work is not quite the same as the man who went out in the morning. The woman who comes home with a full shopping bag is not quite the same as the woman who went out an hour before. We are changed by what we behold, behold *now at this present* . . . and we are changed by all, *now at this present,* by all the multitude of images stored in the deep mind. Hands reach out from the past to shape and mould us in the present hour. What we beheld once upon a time, is not dead and gone, but alive and returning, to do us good or to do us ill. I only wish there were time to expound the massive evidence for what I say. But perhaps there is no need. It is becoming commonplace that childhood experiences can make or mar the adult in middle life.

Even more, there has been a recent disclosure of the fruits of thirty years' research into pre-natal influences, and how they dispose the life pattern, how the moods and emotions of the mother are communicated to the child, how there can be intro-uterine shock, and even terror to the unborn child, and how the echoes of all this, for good or ill, can persist through life.

See then how we are confronted here with life or death. Clearly much of what we may behold is *poison* to us, it may ravage the mind with *obscene images* . . . may *cauterise* the conscience, may *wither* the flower of spiritual perception . . . may pull us down out of the light and beauty of life into the dark and pestilential sewers . . . and so the soul sinks into corruption. But by the same rule, what we behold may be to us *wholesome food* and *healing medicine,* may invest the mind with noble images . . . nourish our taste for the sublime and beautiful, elevate the human spirit to splendid levels of life.

We know it. One television programme will leave us soiled and degraded. Another will leave us with the sense that we have become better men and women.

Thus all these things take us *by both arms* and march us up to that word in our text . . . *we are changed . . .* but in the text . . . all is the upward look, all is the high aspiration, all is the joyful hope.

But we all, with unveiled face, beholding as in a mirror the glory of the Lord . . .

With *unveiled face* . . . the allusion is to Moses. On the heights of the mountain he was in the presence of the Almighty, and there he abode for forty days and forty nights. There he beheld the glory. When he came down, his face shone—he mirrored the glory . . . But the people dared not look upon his face, so he put a veil upon it. But we with unveiled face are to behold the glory . . .

And the glory, what is that? Ah, what can a man say? There in the Scripture it comes with a sense of light and splendour and majesty . . . it is the unutterable beauty . . . it is the flawless purity, the unspeakable love. When *Isaiah* saw it in the Temple he cried out in shame. When *Solomon's priests* sensed it in the Temple they staggered in their courses. When *Ezekiel* saw it, in the plain as he saw it by the River of Chebar, he fell on his face. *When Peter and James and John* saw the glory on Mt. Hermon when Jesus became transfigured before them and His raiment exceeding white as snow, they did not want to go home. Peter proposed building three huts . . . one for the Lord, one for Moses and one for Elijah. *Bless his elated heart!*

When *Paul* saw it on the Damascus Road, he was blind for three days, and a changed man for time and Eternity. I have seen a *group of young people* drop unbidden to their knees one by one, for the weight of the glory, and can hear now the voice of one of them: "O God! O God! O God!"

The glory! *A glimpse* of it will be the highest and best thing a man will see in his life. At another time, he might be enraptured by *great music,* at another time stand still for half an hour on a *mountain top,* at another be near to tears as he watches the beauty and innocency of *little children* at play . . . but to see the glory is *higher* than all these things. A dream! When he sees the glory he will take it into his heart.

But now, *what for us solid citizens,* not much given to visions, perhaps strangers somewhat to the mountain tops of spiritual experience . . . *Where do we look* for a sight of the glory? Paul tells us in the next chapter, he speaks of the *"light of the knowledge of the glory of God in the face of Jesus Christ."* That is where to look, but how to look? Let's get down to cases. It means a portion of your time, and a certain fixity of mind. As you take time for necessary food, and take time for your necessary exercises, so you take time for *beholding the face of Jesus Christ.*

You have your Bible, and you read of how he took hold of the *rotting flesh* of the leper . . . Now behold, now stare, now brood, now ponder. How at that time no one else would do such a thing. He couldn't be any one special to Jesus, because He had only just met him. And then the bewildering thought . . . perhaps every one is special to Jesus . . . Perhaps that is a part of what Divinity is . . . So I also am special to Jesus. He loved me, and gave Himself for me . . . And can it be that I should gain an interest in His blood? Then think of how He did not shrink from touching the loathsomeness . . . Is that not all of a piece—the friend of publicans and sinners . . . Harlots and thieves to you I call . . . the divine stooping to shame, and to pain, and to desolation.

So for ten minutes you behold the glory, and you take into your heart what you see.

And then you arrive at Calvary, for those who know best say that here the *dimmest eye* will see the glory, if only it will look. What's this he says, *Father, forgive them* for they know not what they do . . . How could He do that? These people hated Him, had trapped Him into His doom, even now they are capering about like clowns, and mocking Him as He dies. And He makes Himself, the passionate, pleading counsel for the defence.

And then perhaps you think of the day when you were ravaged with *excruciating pain,* and you couldn't *sleep,* couldn't *read,* couldn't *eat.* All was a terrible *focus* on the pain. But He, He could wrench His thought away from the pain, to these His enemies, and the frightful thing they had brought upon themselves, and long that they should be delivered. Maybe you are baffled, but you are beholding the glory, and taking it into yourself.

Shake your head, maybe, and move on a few verses, and hear the *dying thief* calling across to Jesus: "Lord remember me when Thou comest into Thy Kingdom." What incredible words! The rest . . . some friends, but mostly enemies saw the naked bloodstained contorted Man upon a Cross, but the thief saw a King, perhaps saw the heavenly throne, perhaps legions of angels. Perhaps he saw the Glory. And ponder the superb answer that came ringing back . . . "Today thou shalt be with Me in Paradise." And on that dark and stricken hill, He saw, the Lord Jesus saw, the fair field of Paradise. So we ponder, and behold the glory, and are changed by the same image from glory to glory . . .

And now to finish Paul adds the pregnant words . . . *even by the Spirit of the Lord.* There you are, in your quiet place, alone, you think, with your thoughts, but you are not alone . . . By the simple act of so fixing your gaze, you have moved into the orbit of the Eternal Spirit, and He is there with you, beside you, in you, to further the divine purpose in you. He takes a hand. He is not content to leave this matter to the process of human psychology. He is the Spirit of Light, and He is determined that you will have the light so that you will see what you did not see before . . . He is the Spirit of Understanding . . . and He purposes that you should take more of the ineffable glory into your body, mind, soul and spirit, and grasp and hold what was not yours before. He superintends the work of changing you from glory into glory.

And so the thought races on to the completion of the work, and we know what the purpose is . . . that we should shine among the shining spirits of the Blessed . . . that we should look with unveiled faces upon the unveiled glory, for the glory will not only be all about us, but within us. We shall belong. So:

Turn your eyes upon Jesus,
Look full in His wonderful face,
And the things of earth will grow strangely dim,
In the light of His glory and grace.

GOD LOOKING FOR A MAN

Ezekiel 22:30: And I sought for a man among them, that should build up the wall, and stand in the gap before Me for the land, that I should not destroy it, but I found none.

A MINISTER does well for his congregation and for himself if he can isolate a day from time to time and be away from the manse, and the streets, and the telephone, and get him to the hills. Doubly fortunate he is to have a hill-farmer friend who is to be on the flank of the Pennines that day and will tolerate some amateur help. Perhaps it's dry stone-walling that day. Stand off and look at those walls snaking far up the hillsides. With fell-ponies and sledges, so they say, they got the stones there. Hefting a stone round and round in the hands to see the fit, they would place it unerringly, and reach for another. And not a trowelful of mortar in the lot. Our sheep are Swaledales, an athletic breed. In many a place tall stakes joined by barbed wire march with the walls. Their high-jumping competitions must be curbed. Pity the farmer with a flock of ewes and lambs in a field that marches with the road. If there is a hint of a gap they will find it, and with some hearty pushing and shoving they'll widen it.

So, building up the walls and stopping the gaps, is a stern part of the business.

Ezekiel has much to say about sheep and shepherds, some of it hard to take, and here a vivid image about a fallen wall and a gaping hole takes us far. I do not know how they managed about their sheep-folds in his day, but there must have been two main concerns, one to keep the flocks from wandering, and the other to keep the predators at bay—the lion, the wolf and the bear. A gap in the wall was a sign of spreading destruction. With this image God stamps into the mind of the prophet the disaster creeping upon the nation. There's a gap in the wall, and its vitality is slipping away. There's a gap in the wall, and teeth and claws rend among the flock. So God looks for a man to build up the wall, and to stand in the gap, and He finds none.

We reflect, first of all, that God's search for a man is not always disappointed. Indeed the whole of the Bible-story, and the whole of our Christian history contain the long, long tale of how God found men to build up the wall, and to stand in the gap, a succession of men from the dim beginnings of history, a succession of men not to be counted, to build up walls not to be reckoned, and to stand in gaps not to be numbered. O, I know it buffets the mind—how can it be that out of the invisible, from beyond the veil, there can come the clear ringing call that roots a mortal, earthly man to the spot where he stands, so that this creature of a day knows beyond cavil, beyond doubt, knows in his blood and bones, that he is now under the hand of the Almighty God and deputised for a duty.

God says: "I sought for a man," and we see at once that this is God's method. If there is an enterprise to be begun and furthered, God looks for a man. We do not say that God is confined to this, but this is His familiar way. Any educated man could give dozens of examples off the cuff. Give him time, and he could give you hundreds. And those that delve into the matter could give you thousands. And then there are those who probe into particular periods of religious history, and they come back with names one has never heard of. Or someone will have a mind to write the history of missions in some obscure place, and now you get a list of names that trip the tongue. Or a minister will move to a new charge, and he will talk to old folk who have long memories, and root in cupboards stuffed with yellowing papers, and it will seem as if they come marching out of the past, men and women, not known beyond this neighbourhood, but here God called them and here they built up the wall and here they stood in the gap; they laboured, and he is entered into their labours.

God calls and men answer, and when they do we can begin to trace what fell out from that call and that answer. William Carey was called, and the gap in the wall for him was India, so the village shoemaker becomes Professor of Sanskrit. He sets up printing-presses. The Bibles are on their way to the cities and villages of India. He deploys a growing band of missionaries. God looked for Wilberforce and found him, and you know what fell out from that: and the Earl of Shaftesbury and what fell out from that. And John Wesley, and George Fox and Martin Luther, and D. L. Moody, and David Livingstone. I am a fool to begin, for I can never end, and there is no convenient place for me to pause. With all these and with many more we can show how God sought and found them, and how they built up the walls and how they stood in the gaps. Cause and effect we can show. God's method, God's purpose, abundantly displayed, abundantly illustrated. The mystic and mysterious call, out of the sky, out of the blue heavens, out of the invisible. Of this we can paint no picture, make no model, but what issues from it is solid in history, ever evolving, ever spreading, spreading now so that no single brain can take it in, but really there, as plain to the sight as a cathedral or a hospital, as lively as a praising, praying congregation, as hard-working as all the charities of Christian love.

But our text is not of the men God found. Our text is of the man who was not found, and of the wall that was never built up, and of the gap that was never filled. How are we to think of that, much less speak of it? God looked for a man, sought for a man, searched for a man. God lit His candle, and went abroad. O, there were men in plenty, but not all would have the physique for it, and even less would have the brain for it, but surely the light of the candle would travel over the faces of not a few, strong enough in frame and astute enough in mind, but seemingly there was not one amongst them who had the heart for it. God called this one and that, but none answered. Now all this is thickly veiled from our sight. We can tell many a tale of those who heard the call, and made answer. Our story books are full of accounts of those who heard the knocking of the Divine knuckles upon the heart's door, and were swift to lift the latch. But where are the stories of those who heard the knocking but did not move a muscle? 'Tis all hidden, all hidden.

Hidden also are the consequences that flowed from the stony face and the stony heart. Clearly some wall is fallen still, and some gap unfilled. Where? Who knows where? But let us move away from metaphor, and consider some blighted piece of human existence, say a notorious criminal family, or some sector of a city where all manner of evil is spawned, or a tribe or a nation where evil men rule an evil people, and then see how far it is possible to link the present mischief with some past neglect. It cannot be done. Historians have sought to explain the fall of empires by pointing to the decay of virtue in previous generations, but it is the kind of thing that lies outside the strict canons of scientific inquiry.

Psychiatric literature, probing into the origins of mental disorder and wondering about inheritance, quotes the famous case of Ada Jurke, a notorious drinking woman, who had 709 known descendants, of whom 106 were illegitimate, 142 beggars, 64 supported by their township, 181 prostitutes, and 76 convicted criminals (7 of them murderers). "But," say Henderson and Gillespie, "it seems unwarranted to attribute this entirely to the alcoholism of Ada." Unwarranted indeed! We may remain suspicious, but to establish an intellectually convincing linkage between the last case and the first is impossible. Even if we could, we still have not shown that this human wretchedness and misery stemmed from some refusal of the call of God.

How, then, is this Scripture with its tragedy and pathos to lay a forcible grip upon our minds? I confess that, as I read it, I hear a sob in the voice of God. I confess to a picture in my mind of God, lifting up His candle to face after face, and His face is the face of the Man of Sorrows. "I found none!" and the despair of it flows like a dark wave through the universe. How, then, are we to come near to the heart of God in this matter?

First, I think, by imagination. There is at least one case in the Gospels of one who seemingly heard the call and refused it. His name we do not know. We speak of him as the Rich Young Ruler. You remember? He wanted to know how he might inherit eternal life. Jesus told him to sell all that he had and give to the poor, and come, follow Him. And he went away sorrowful for he had great possessions. The last we see of him is a retreating back. But, of course, we cannot chop off our thinking there. What became of the lad? Did he sit up late that night, and afterward toss and turn on his bed? And what when the midday darkness fell on Calvary? Was he there? And what when the electrifying rumour ran, the rumour of the Resurrection? Was he on the streets and in the crowd at Pentecost? We do not know. It could well be that there was an hour when he piled his riches into a trust fund for the poor, and then, slimmed down and travelling light, joined the increasing thousands who were pledged to the eternal service.

Thus it might be, for all I know, that a saga was written of his faith and devotion and heroism, but, if so, such a record was lost. So all I can see is a retreating back. Contrariwise it could be that he went on to spend his life and his talents in multiplying his great possessions, and in the end became like that man of whom Jesus spoke who came to the point where he was rich and increased with goods, built bigger barns, and told his soul to take it easy, who one midnight heard his bedroom-door creak, and a voice that said: "This night is thy soul required of thee." But if this last was the truth of that rich young ruler, I have no picture at all of what happened in this place and that, or of what failed to happen in this place and that because he retreated from Christ. And thus when I read that God sought for a man and found none, I feel the prick, but I do not feel the stab. So in the General Confession: "We have done those things which we ought not to have done" and for those things there is a time and place, and an ugly shape and horrid colours, but when we go on to sins of omission . . . "left undone those things which we ought to have done" there is a vagueness and no outline. Where it is things we have done, conscience cuts to the bone, where it is things omitted, a mere scratch on the skin.

Now this ought not to be. So again I summon my imagination to the stern work. I allow it to pervert the Bible story. You remember Isaiah in the Temple, and the voice that said: "Whom shall I send and who will go for us?" and how the prophet said: "Here am I, send me?" Then the vandal in my imagination will not have it so. I make Isaiah into the man that was not found. He heard and he feared. And fearing, he stiffened every muscle, and kept his gaze on the tesselated pavement. He told himself he was not to be swayed by emotion, and that great commitments deserved careful consideration. So he waited until the moment passed and his pulse was steady. Then he went home.

The next thing I do is to snip out of Acts Eight the tale of the eunuch of Ethiopia, for that tale pivots on the man's reading of the Fifty-Third of Isaiah, but if Isaiah had not said, "Here am I, send me," there was no Prophecy of Isaiah, and no Fifty-Third. And to be robbed of that is to be robbed indeed. And then there was a genius of the eighteenth century who interwove great words with great music, and one can hear it world-wide, over the airwaves, from great halls, great choirs, great orchestras. And millions, many of them grieved, distraught, despairing, lift up their heads and lift up their hearts when they hear it, clear and ringing: "Comfort ye, comfort ye, My people, saith your God." I must wipe out all that with a rag, wet with angels' tears, if so be that Isaiah was a man not found.

It is this dearth, this famine of hearing of the words of the Lord, the fallen unlifted, the hungry unfed, the sick untended, the lost not found, which is all the sorrow in God's cry when He says: "I found none."

But now, the Scripture might not bite deep enough for some, because what Ezekiel reports is remote in time, and place and circumstance. So I refer you to a book the Methodists of the British Isles publish every year, the Minutes of the Conference. It includes the names and the stations of the ministers. Flicking over the pages I come to the Africa Stations. There you have the names of each locality where a minister is required, and cheek by jowl with it the name of the men appointed or the terse expression, "One wanted." I give a brief selection. Ivory Coast District; one wanted at Grand Bassam-ville; one wanted at Abobo-Gare; one wanted at Songon-Agban; one wanted at N'Douci; and so on down the page and over the page in a tragic litany. You may, if you will, see it as a dry, toneless, official list; but if you have ears to hear you might hear the cry of Almighty God: "I sought for a man that should build up the wall at Kilibo, and stand in the gap; but I found none."

O, God searched! He lit His candle and the flame of it illumined many a face, and there was many a one with the physique for it, and many a one with the brain for it, and many a one with the courage for it, but none with the heart for it. Many and many a one He called, but "they all with one consent began to make excuse." And I toy with the thought that somewhere in a Methodist Church there is a man, now in middle-age, doing fairly well in business, and yeoman work in his church, and he and his wife are making a good job of bringing up their children, but really he ought to be at Kilibo, building up the wall, and standing in the gap.

But there, do you see, I might have compounded the remoteness of the text in speaking of Kilibo, so far off—to most of us a mere name. But already we have been invaded by the notion that there is no one particular wall, no one particular gap, but there have been and are broken-down walls innumerable, gaps that cannot be counted, and the grim certainty that some of the walls that stand today will be breached tomorrow. We may have a sense of being overfaced, and from that there may spring paralysis.

The first thought to me is that if there are so many breaches, so many gaps, then a portion of them will be about me, here in this place. lying at my gate, and they will be here now, while I think. They could be labelled with my own postal code. It may be that you have thought about this one and that before.

It may be that the light of God's candle is on your face at this moment. Right. Slip off your jacket. Roll up your sleeves. Bend. Take up a fallen stone. Heft it about to see how it is going to fit. Push it in, easing it gently, to firm it. And God has found another to build up a wall, and to stand in a gap.

(Note: The brow of the reader of this sermon might be wrinkled at this place and that, unless he knows it was preached to an assembly of ministers).

THE SOWING OF THE LIGHT

Psalm 97 : 11 : Light is sown for the righteous . . .

THERE seems to be something wrong here. I say it again. Light is sown for the righteous. Ah! yes. The noun and the verb don't go together. We try for the picture of someone sowing light and the picture won't come. Sowing seed, yes, the basket encircled with the left arm, the right hand dipping, coming up with a fistful, sweeping and scattering. That's easy . . . But sowing light? No. It won't come. So we go through half a dozen translations, to see if somebody has made something else of the Hebrew. But no, they are all the same. A certain Dr. Briggs gives us pause. A man of massive mind was Dr. Briggs and wrote a massive commentary. He feels it doesn't make sense and suspects some corruption in the text. So I am forced back on the Hebrew. Sure enough . . . that's what it says. Light is sown for the righteous.

Now brooding upon this mystery, we see that this righteous man is not said *himself* to sow the light. No! No! If he sows anything . . . he sows his righteous deeds, thoughts, words. I can get that picture . . . as if the seeds flying from that scattering hand have each a name . . . this is love, and this is kindness, and this is courage, and this is compassion, and as if each such seed fructifies in the rich soil of human experience, and as if there is a harvest, each according to its kind. That I can see. But the text says that light is sown *for* him. As if some other agency is at work, as if some other power or process or person contrives that in parallel with his sowing of righteousness there is a sowing of another kind, invisible, completely unseen, yet marching, scattering with a sowing of light for his own peculiar and particular harvest.

We are on to something exciting here, part of that general excitement that has always thrilled in human life, the thrill of discovery, the breaking out of the secrets of the universe. This has been called the age of science . . . but there never has been an age that was not the age of science. When some far-off ancestor discovered the use of the bow and arrow the age of science had already begun . . . see him go on . . . he finds the best kind of wood for his bow, and the best size, and then the arrow, straight and smooth the shaft, the best kind of bar and how to feather it for a straight shoot, and how to allow for the wind, and the dropping shot. In fact the laws of archery . . . And then he began to tease out the laws of agriculture . . . and the laws of medicine, how best to deal with wounds and fevers . . . So that out there, in the wide world of this day, the pursuit of knowledge is vast . . . the laws of almost every conceivable thing are being pursued—mechanics, engineering, chemistry, physiology, botany . . . but the list is endless. Men want to know what is the case, how does it work, what are the facts? Nay, my wife bought a paperback on jam-making this week (with my full approval: I am all for jam). Out of a multitude of experiments, and out of wide experience they gather the laws . . . for this kind of fruit and that, how to prepare, how long to boil . . . That is science . . . and there is an immense amount of science in the kitchen.

And here in this place we have our own science, and the most enthralling science of all, the science of the spiritual life . . . the laws of the traffic between this world and the world unseen. What is the cause of the communion between God and man? What are the facts? How does it work? What we are told in the Book of God, and how it is displayed in the vast experimentation of the spiritual life. Early on we are given a vivid picture in Jacob's dream of a ladder set up between heaven and earth, and angels ascending and descending upon it. And after that the Bible is full of it. The to and fro of the divine and human commerce. The swinging tides of the spiritual life. The signal flashed from the earth . . . and the answering signal out of heaven.

We distinguish certain elements. Best known is prayer. More thought about than any other, stirring the mind with many questions, and still charged with mystery; but to the experienced Christian there is a conviction solid and unquestioned . . . He knows his prayer is heard . . . sometimes he's sensed the Presence, and sometimes he does not, but he knows his prayer is heard. Sometimes his prayer is answered as he wants, and sometimes as he does not expect, sometimes it seems that God says No. Sometimes that God bids him wait. But he knows his prayer is heard. If anyone doubts the power of prayer read the life of George Müller of Bristol.

Another element is in giving. Give, it says, and it shall be given unto you . . . And he that soweth sparingly shall reap also sparingly, and he that soweth bountifully shall reap also bountifully . . . You cannot even give a cup of cold water to a disciple . . . but somewhere along the trail you receive a reward . . . The law is fixed. It regulates the traffic between God and man.

Once again, but not so familiar, with praise and thanksgiving. You might think that when the great hymn is raised in the church of God, sounding out the brimming gratitude of the people, you might think that the terminus of such praise is the heavenly place . . . and there it rests . . . but no! there into the unseen the wave flows in its thanksgiving, but *from* there the wave ebbs back to the people in grace and blessing and glory. There is Scripture for that in many a hint to those who can catch on, and in many a word for those who have ears to hear.

Now here in the text is something of the same style, of the same genus, of the same unalterable law. Light is sown for the righteous. The psalmist has his eye upon the righteous man . . . perhaps some fellow he knows well, been in his house often enough, gossiped with him in the fields, watched him with an affectionate eye, and he has the measure of the man. There was that time when a stranger travelling through the village fell sick, and he had him in his house at once. They nursed him day and night until the fever abated, and insisted that he stay until his strength came back. And then the regular visits to old Joachim in the croft at the end of the lane, always with something in his hand, and always time for a gossip with the old man. And the mothers of the place had long ago given up telling their little ones not to bother him. Bothering Mr. Righteous was an institution, and he had only himself to blame. You have a glimpse of the man? Light, said the psalmist, is sown for him. And light in due time he will reap.

But, you ask, what is this light that this man reaps?

I wish I could tell you. I wish I could tell myself. I think I am dazzled by the light itself. I read that God dwelleth in light that no man can approach unto, and I suspect that all any man can know here below is a few broken gleams of that light. A friend of mine was telling me how he was on holiday in the Isle of Wight, and how he was introduced to an astronomer, and visited the man's home, and there in the garden a companion made as if he would look at the sun through the telescope, when a blow from the astronomer sent him flying. A merciful blow . . . for that intensified light would have made him blind. Broken gleams only, while we are here on earth.

We see certain *parallels* with the *light of the sun.* Says Jesus, he that followeth Me shall not walk in darkness but shall have the light of life (John 8). Ever been in a strange place on a *pitch black night* without a torch, your boots feeling for the hollows and the bumps, and your hands out for the tree or the hedge. It's hard going and slow going, and how d'you know you'll get where you want to be? Are there not times when a man's life is exactly that? Who am I and why am I here? Was I meant for something? Is there some intentioned destiny? In which direction should I aim my life? Suppose I make a scheme . . . Do not the best laid schemes of mice and men gang aft agley? It's like trying to make your way in the dark . . . but here is the promise. He that followeth Me, says Jesus, shall not walk in darkness. And that links with an older promise . . . In all thy ways acknowledge Him and He shall direct thy paths . . . and make with a testimony from far back. Thy word is a lamp unto my feet and a light unto my path. That is a light sown for the righteous. Sure guidance through the shadowy unknown of this world.

May we not see another parallel in *photosynthesis?* Everybody knows by now that the light of the sun is the food of plants; they grow by the grace of the sunshine. The vast harvests of the world which feed its vast population, derive from that incandescent orb 93 million miles away. What did you eat to-day? Now the Bible has much to say about growth in grace . . . the aim and object is that we are to be full-grown men, according to the measure of the stature of the fullness of Christ. And over the centuries by a consensus of those who know best, certain men and women have come to a rare beauty of life. By what food have they been nourished? By the light. Christ says that He is the light of the world. He also says that He is the bread that comes down from heaven. The mystic light is the mystic bread, and by that light which is bread men grow to manhood in Christ.

There is another parallel that I see. And many of you will see it too. You will see it, because it has fallen to you to know the night of pain. The dim light over the nurse's desk. The quiet step of the night sister on her rounds. The heavy breath of your fellow sufferers. But no sleep for you. Of course they gave you something to help you sleep, but the pain fought it off . . . and you lie there while the moments go by on leaden feet. You know all that. Or maybe for some others not pain of body but pain of heart . . . the long and lonely hours of intolerable grief. But then, d'you remember, the lightening of the darkness beyond the uncurtained windows, and then soon afterwards, the reddening on a floating cloud, and the dawn has come. O the blessed relief! Why? someone will say, was the pain, the grief the less? No! No! But somehow it was easier to bear.

So is the mystic light . . . it is the comfort wherewith we are comforted of God. We are stronger to bear, stronger to battle on, and when the thing is over, we know, and there is no question that there was light for us in the dark valley.

O, yes! Light is sown for the righteous . . .

Now it is possible that someone here is stirring restlessly at this exposition of the text. Introspectiveness, that is the burden of the complaint. Encouraging each of us to a preoccupation with his own soul. We shut the heavy doors against the world outside and occupy ourselves with personal piety. But outside is the real world, the world of recession, of unemployment, of riots in the streets, of packed prisons and bullets and bombs . . . and further afield, the ravage of war in this place and that, massacre here and starvation there. And here you dwell on the niceties of a translation from the Hebrew. Can you not hear the children cry for bread?

I answer, Yes, I can hear the children cry for bread . . . I have heard them with these ears, and the sound is unforgettable. And if anyone here is angry with me, I love him for it, for I know the anger springs from his concern. *But now hear me!*

The light of which I speak is not for *personal use only.* It is never marked *Not Transferable.* We are not to put it under a *bed,* but set it up to give light to all that are in the house. The light of a lighthouse is not given so that the lighthouse keeper may read his book, but so that it may pierce the fog and sweep out over the dark seas. Years ago, when I was stationed in York, I received a telephone message that called me at once over the Pennines to the west coast. I hadn't gone far when I realised that the generator of my car was on the blink, and my only light was in a fading battery. So I crawled slowly along until I was overtaken by blazing headlights then I would open the throttle and tuck myself in behind, travelling by another's light. When he swung off, I must perforce crawl again until some more blazing headlights overtook me. So I made my way until I dropped into the sleeping towns of Lancashire with the amber lights still burning in the streets. So I came to where I was needed, and spoke with my mother before she died. Travelling by the lights of others. So every man who harvests the light will travel by that light, but he will also lend that light for other benighted pilgrims.

One thing more about light which I throw out for you to ruminate about. You know how you may see in the distance, a glow of light in the sky . . . you know at once what it is . . . the lights of a town reflected from the clouds. Or how you can walk at night down a suburban road, and you walk not only by the light of the street lamps, but by the glow through the curtains from many a house. I am thinking of diffused light, refracted and reflected light, how light spreads beyond the direct beam. Consider what would happen if you took a large map of the world and ransacking history for every instance of something wrought, created or invented which lifted the life of humanity whether it be in philosophy, in science, in art, or in humanitarianism, and then you pin a coloured flag in every place where such a thing sprang forth. Now my guess is that while those flags might be spread abroad, there would be a crowded cluster within the bounds of historic Christendom. After that the argument would start, arguments about our temperate climate, our inheritance from the Golden Age of Greece, and much else. But I offer this . . . that where the Gospel light is shining, there is not only the vivid blaze of immediate illumination, but there is a diffusion, reflection and refraction over a broader scene.

I understand that it is good science that when a man bounces a ball on the ground, the ball not only goes to meet the earth, but the earth comes up to meet the ball. I have heard that when a man shouts, the waves of sound go out and out beyond the far borders of the further galaxies. It may well be that when a man lights a match he illuminates the universe.

So then Light is sown for the righteous, and our immediate duty is plain . . . to go out in that troubled world and play the part of righteous men and women, and to play that part not simply because of the following harvest of light, but because in any event right is right and must be done, because always right is better than wrong, and kindness is better than cruelty, and giving is better than grasping and love is better than hating.

They say that honesty is the best policy . . . but sometimes the portion of the honest men has been the prison, the rack, the scaffold. There are times when the tyrant with the heart of a devil is on the throne, and the righteous must fly to the hills, or the boats, or the dens and caves of the earth . . . But it is better to stand on the scaffold with the right, than to share the throne with wickedness . . . Our business is to play the part of the righteous in the name of Him whose righteousness brought Him to the Cross.

And if we would be righteous there is a multitude of models for our example. From the New Testament onwards, I despair to recite the names Saint Francis and Saint Caterinetta of Sienna. Claver of Carthage, Father Damien of Molokai. Wesley, Wilberforce and Shaftesbury. Andrew Bonar and Murray McCheyne. In our own days Schweitzer of Lambarene, and Kagawa of Tokio, Mother Teresa of Calcutta . . . Above all remember Him on whom all the saints have fixed their eyes . . . Jesus Christ the Lord, the Rose of Sharon, the Lily of the Valley, the fairest among ten thousand. Follow in His steps . . . for He has said: "He that followeth Me shall not walk in darkness but shall have the light of life."

AMAZING GRACE

2 Cor. 13 : 14 : The grace of the Lord Jesus Christ.

AMAZING GRACE! and how amazing it was when someone from the pop culture, where they are always bustling after something new, counting yesterday's songs as dead as yesterday's news, should suddenly reach back, beyond our fathers, and beyond their fathers, and snatch a song out of a fossilised day, and carry that song to the top of the pops. Amazing grace! it swept abroad like a musical gale of wind. It came over the air, stamped on a million discs, sung by soloist, sung by choirs, recorded by the pipes and drums of a dragoon regiment. Old fashioned, Bible rooted words, to an old fashioned tune.

Grace is a dear familiar word to us, glancing and gleaming through the New Testament, threading through our prayers, dancing in our hymns. Would it not be well if we should bring some depth of pondering to the word?

There is indeed something mildly comical in making the venture in a single sermon. For this word of one syllable carries enormous freight. What do they say? —a portmanteau word, a pantechnicon word, nay, an ocean-going cargo ship of a word. Many books could not exhaust its meaning, and ten thousand saints could not prove it all. But we make the venture, for half a loaf, even a crumb, is better than no bread.

Grace is the translation of the Greek word *charis,* and there we must begin. When first we see it spring into the language, it meant that which affords joy, pleasure, delight, that which has charm, sweetness, lowliness, and it still holds that meaning in our own tongue. We see it in the movement of a horse running wild, in an otter twisting and turning in the water, in the swoop of a bird. And seeing such a thing we kindle to it. Watching athletics, we see some lumbering strongly to the tape, others pounding mightily, but here and there we see a runner or a hurdler, with a free flowing movement, and we have a sense of beauty in motion. That is grace.

From that original meaning, it flowed over to other things, for men had the same feeling for the attractive elegance in noble forms of speech, for when a thing is fitly said we sense the same kind of beauty in the graceful movement of the words. And so to taste and elegance in dress, and to refinement in manner and courtesy.

This root meaning of something beautiful never departs from the word grace. Grace from a thing displayed harks back to *the mind and spirit of a man who displays it.*

Thus you know that the institution of slavery disfigured the social life of that ancient day, and with it went much cruelty. But here and there would be a man who had his own kindly way with his slaves, like that Roman centurion who begged Jesus to come and heal his slave. Such a man would count himself a father to them, feed them well, care for them in sickness, watch over them in old age. Such a man was said to have grace . . . they could see the gleam of beauty in that man's spirit.

Years ago a Congregational minister told me a tale. He was once stationed in Aberdeen, and it fell to him on a day to conduct a pauper's funeral. They were about to begin the committal. The coffin of cheap wood was lying by the open grave; no flowers, no mourners. Then he heard the slow tramp of many feet. Through the cemetery gates came a large procession. He understood. The funeral of a notable lady of those parts, a countess. Then suddenly the procession stopped. The Earl took a wreath from his wife's coffin, came over to the pauper's grave, and laid the wreath down. Stood for a moment, bareheaded, head bowed, and then returned, and the procession moved on. And that was grace, grace in a gesture that spoke grace in the spirit of a man.

Says the Apostle John : "We beheld His glory, the glory as of the only begotten of the Father, full of grace and truth" . . . the glory shot through with gleams of the holy beauty.

There was a man whose tale I would have loved to hear from his own lips. "You see we had heard of this Jesus up there in the caves of the hills. We'd heard that He had healed blind people and paralysed and such like. Some of the others were cynical. They said He'd never come within fifty yards of us lepers. But I thought there was a slim chance and I took it. I hid behind a rock until He came abreast, and then I hobbled out. The others backed off, but He stood His ground. I knelt at His feet, and put in my prayer. He spoke me kindly, and then, and then I felt His grip on my arm, just there, you see. I couldn't believe it. I stared at the rotten skin between the brown fingers, and then I looked up at His face. I'll remember the look on His face, and feel the grip of His fingers to my dying day. And the man would dab at the tears that ran down his cheeks. He had seen divine beauty in a face and divine beauty in a gesture.

That was what the Apostle John meant . . . full of grace . . . something that caught at the heart, and started the tears.

Paul saw it in the cosmic seep of things (2 Cor. 8 :9). "The grace of our Lord Jesus Christ who though He was rich, yet for your sakes became poor." Dwells on it later.

"Made Himself of no reputation, and took upon Him the form of a servant, being made in the likeness of men."

The pre-existent Prince of Glory, deserted the light and splendour of the heavenly palaces, divested Himself of all that and took upon Him the form of flesh, for the dust of the road, and the flogging before the praetorium, and the dragging horror of the via dolorosa, and the piercing of the nails . . . for your sakes, for your sakes . . . Amazing grace! Amazing grace!

But now the word goes on to further enrichment. It is not only a beauty enshrined in the heart of a man or the heart of God. It is not only a visible deed shining with beauty. It is an effectual working power. It is the loveliness of love at work, in action, throbbing with power.

We have clues enough in the physical world of the meaning of power. There is power in the sun and the wind, in the tides and in fire. Such power can both bless and curse. The melting snows on the mountainside can flow down to irrigate the thirsty land, or sweep down to overflow the rivers, and carry all before them. The sun can ripen the corn, or wither the fruitful plants. The wind can drive the windmills or devastate the land. Thus the forward progress of man depends on his skill to harness the power.

Now the power of grace is different. It can only bless, can never curse . . . But is a power . . . a power that can create beauty, but never ugliness. A power that can heal but never hurt. Politicians now speak threateningly of famine of physical power. But the power of grace is unstinted, ever available. Part of the poverty of the third world is a lack of physical power. But no man in any place need lack the power of grace. The house of a man's soul may indeed be dark and destitute behind the locked doors, the drawn curtains, the barred shutters, but the throbbing power of grace is ever flowing round his house, searching for any chink or crack through which it may come.

It can work in odd ways. Paul had some physical infirmity and prayed thrice to be delivered from it, but he was not delivered from it. God said: "My grace is sufficient for thee," as if to say, My grace will override all impediments, carry you and your infirmity, it will not brook any defeat, but carry you with a high hand to victory after victory. It is sufficient. It is always enough and more than enough.

But if you would catch a glimpse of the kind of work this power achieves, imagine some sculptor of excellence at work on a misshapen lump of stone, seamed with all manner of impurity . . . who means when he is finished to have carved an angel. Or think of a plastic surgeon, and on the table before him someone hideously scarred by fire. Lying ahead of him is one operation after another, and another, and another, but in his mind's eye the surgeon sees the man restored to his family and society. Nay, he will not be as a Greek god, but he'll pass muster, more than pass muster.

Isaiah puts it beautifully: "In the wilderness shall waters break and streams in the desert, yea, the desert shall rejoice and blossom as the rose."

I remember from years ago having supper with a man who had spent most of his years in jail. Some of his crimes had been savage and brutal, and the marks were still on his features. He told me that during his last sentence, he had been bored sitting in solitary, and picked up a Bible the Gideons had provided . . . flipped over the pages carelessly, and then his attention held he began to read. The upshot was that he found Christ in his cell.

I knew that the past four years he had been a man transformed. But what moved me was the look on his face as he spoke of the Lord Jesus. There was something beautiful that overlaid the brutal features, beautiful, I thought, in its radiance. That is the work of grace, miracle-working grace, being beautiful itself, its work is beauty.

"To bring many sons unto glory" . . . so it is written . . . but think of the sons as it begins its work, with ugly things in the heart, and ugly things in the mind, ugly things spat from the tongue, men with an ugly past that won't let them go. And grace goes forth to bring them to glory, to make them splendid and beautiful among the angels in heaven, arrayed in white robes and palms in their hands. Only grace would dare to begin, and only grace could carry it through. Amazing Grace!

And finally something we dare not leave out, for the Good Book is full of it. Grace is free. "Fear not little flock, it is your Father's good pleasure to give you the Kingdom. Freely ye have received. If ye, then, being evil, know how to give good gifts to your children, how much more shall your heavenly Father give the Holy Spirit to them that ask Him . . . He that spared not His only Son, but delivered Him up for us all, how shall He not with Him, freely give us all things? By grace are ye saved, and that through faith; not of yourselves, it is the gift of God. The wages of sin is death, but the gift of God is eternal life."

What a battle it is to get this Gospel truth home to the heart! What persuasiveness of the preacher, and what persuasiveness of the Holy Ghost, to settle this truth into the deep inside of a man! For perceive how enmeshed we are with the notion of deserving . . . how everything conspires to get that word deserving into our blood and our bone. When we are little . . . If you are a good boy . . . but if you are naughty . . . and of course quite properly . . . And then in the courts of justice . . . the careful scrupulous weighing the good against the bad. And certainly in the academic examination . . . the thing well done, on the one hand, the thing done ill on the other, and so in employment, and so on the playing field, with a book that is written, with a drama that is played, with a song that is sung . . . always the balancing, the good against the bad, the worthy against the unworthy . . . And so the reward according to the balance . . . what he deserves.

And then added to that. Ticket-holders only, pay at the door? Are you a member? Show your passport. So to all our solidly conditioned souls, comes this flaming word of the Gospel . . . Free grace, free forgiveness, free salvation, the road to God wide open to every man.

Sometimes when I have found this truth baffling to get into my soul again, I have thought of our own John Wesley climbing the scaffold at Tryham with a man about to die, and while the grisly preparations were going on, talking persuasively to the man with his field Bible open in his hand. Did that man deserve heaven? Not he. Did he now have time to put things right, to do enough good, to balance all the years of evil? Did he have time for some sacred pilgrimage? Time to consult with a priest? No. Time only to say: "God be merciful to me, a sinner," time only to receive the free grace, swift as light into his heart.

Or, if it will help, think of this. A woman I know was on her way to see her elderly mother, with a bunch of flowers. Her road took her through a mean street. Coming towards her was a bedraggled old woman—you saw more of them in those days—the old woman's face lightened as she saw the flowers, and she said, "Ain't they lovely?" The other replied, "Yes, they are, and they're for you," thrust them into the other's hand and passed on looking for another flower shop.

A free gift those flowers just like grace . . . and like the flowers grace is beautiful.

NO MAN IS AN ISLAND

Rom. 14:7: For none of us liveth to himself.

NONE of us! Not even Robinson Crusoe! If anyone appeared isolated, remote from the outside world, he did. But, as the story fell out, his crops, his plantations and his herds, wrought in those lonely years on the islands, were life-savers for other men at a later time. John Donne said at an earlier time that no man is an island . . . and not even, it seems, when he lives on an island. Now a broad truth of that kind needs breaking down into its component parts, and this we shall shift to do.

See this, first, that some animals are *loners.* Spiders strike me as loners, and so do butterflies. Ants and bees are not so; they live in armies or swarms. I think of tigers and leopards as loners . . . but deer, buffalo, giraffe, and elephant congregate in herds. What kind of a creature is man? A herd-creature without question! We are gregarious. We vary a bit within the tribe; thus this one and that will take pleasure in a long day's walk alone. Others much prefer to be with the crowd, but we are creatures of the herd. Now the *code* of the herd is important. With animals it seems fairly simple and stable. Thus a herd of springboks is quietly grazing when a doe on the fringe suddenly takes off at high speed. The rest of the herd do not call a committee to discuss the strange behaviour of Gertrude. The rest of the herd takes off at high speed. It is part of the code.

The human code of the herd is immensely complicated, and varies from place to place, but the pressure to obey it is always enormous. Deep-rooted in all of us is the urge to avoid the displeasure and to gain the praise of the herd. It may be our own local and particular part of the herd, our clique, our set, our gang . . . but it's mighty strong. So already we are in the grip of forces which will shape our behaviour and mould our personalities. No man lives to himself.

A *mode* of this obedience is seen in imitation. If you wish your chimpanzee to take tea out of a cup, you have simply to take tea out of a cup when he is watching. Put down the cup and out will come a hairy hand, and up the cup will go to his lips. But do not feel superior. Only take care that you do not imitate him. Hanging from a branch by one hand can cause comment. For you also are an imitator. We grow by imitation. We learn by imitation. Some men arrive on the heights by imitation. Some men arrive in the gutter by imitation.

When I was at school we wore caps. How else, when walking abroad, could we signify our respect for any masters we met? Certain lewd fellows of the baser sort thought it would be a ploy, not merely to touch the peak, but to raise the cap with a sweeping gesture when they met a master. But most of the masters of that day were ex-army officers of the First World War, and trained experts in dealing with dumb insolence. However, there was a prefect called Dickinson. He was Victor Ludorum and wing three-quarter in the first fifteen. It would have been a sight to see Seb. Coe trying to catch him. Now Dickinson wore his cap, not square on his head like a guardsman, nor on the back of his head like certain graceless fighter-pilots I once knew, but pulled down over his right eye in a sinister fashion. More sinister over the left eye? Need I tell you that every fag in the first form wore his cap pulled down over the right eye?

Imitation is one of the mighty lords of human behaviour; and, where admiration is fixed, imitation is strong.

Still on this theme that no man lives to himself . . . consider how much each of us is a prey to the emotions of others. The experts have long brooded over the fact, evolved theories about it and given it technical names: but look at the thing itself. If, passing down the street, you come across three people staring into the sky, and one says: "There it is." Another says: "I wonder what it is?" Then their inquisitiveness will stir the subtle emotion of curiosity in you, and you will swing your gaze upwards. Or picture me reading a book at my fireside. Something in the book amuses me. I begin to chuckle. Then the full absurdity seizes me, and I begin to laugh, then in a moment the book is down on my knees and I am shaking like a jelly. My wife, who is on the other side of the fireplace, darning my socks, a humourless business, begins to titter, and then to laugh . . . though she does not know the joke. Or it falls to me, as it often falls to a minister, to conduct a funeral service for somebody I have never known, but as the sounds and signs of heartbreak come to me from the front pew, I find a lump come into my throat. And perhaps with you as I spoke of laughing, there was a ripple of amusement within you, and when I spoke of the funeral, it was replaced by a sense of the solemn.

Now your minds are multiplying instances. Someone in a theatre catches a whiff of burning, panics, cries "Fire," and the word and the panic rushes all round the theatre. There's a scramble for the exits and grievous damage is done. There's a scuffle in the streets involving some toughs and the police . . . the anger and the hatred spread through the streets, and a neighbourhood is ablaze with riot.

And so we learn the lesson. There seems to be no defence against invading emotions, and emotions are the great energisers of human behaviour. And no man, *no man,* lives unto himself.

A fourth factor I offer, but do not press, for your consideration. I mean the unassisted transmission of thought from one mind to another. It used to be called "telepathy," but so many strange things happened in the experiments that now they prefer to call it "Extra Sensory Perception." For myself, I am convinced. I think I have read pretty widely in the growing volume of literature, and have carried out one or two simple experiments myself, on animals as well as humans, but I press my convictions on no man.

I suggest to you, however, that no longer may we think of thought as something locked in the mind until it is released by voice or pen or some other signal, but thought itself can be a transmitted thing, and that there is another gate, besides the gate of the senses by which thought, not our own, may enter in.

And the possibility yet to be demonstrated, that waking or sleeping, each of us is transmitting and receiving thought, soundlessly and invisibly. Moreover, we already know that thoughts are potent, and thoughts effect change.

In the face of all this, we have to look two ways. First, at ourselves. I do not live unto myself. I am not an island. Everywhere and always what I am, what I think, do, and say, are affecting other people. I talk with a stranger for five minutes and he passes on subtly changed and different because of me. But what sort of change? What sort of difference? We all know that there are some people who travel through life leaving a trail of destruction behind them, and you can mark their track by tears and hurt and heartbreak. It is not only what they do but what they are and what they are is a disease which infects other people. And we all know that some who travel through life leave a blessing where they go. These are the creators, the healers, the givers, and again it is not only by what they do, but by what they are. Theirs is the infection of a good courage, of compassion, of faith and hope and love.

And that's a choice each of us has to make. We can't contract out of it. It belongs to the nature of things. What I am is either going to lift others, or throw them down. I can bless or curse human lives. I can heal or hurt, and it all depends on what I am, what I am in my mind and heart, what I am in the sight of God.

Now, looking beyond ourselves, we see that from birth to death innumerable hands are busy trying to shape and mould us into this pattern and that. "Leave me alone!" is a feeble and hopeless cry. They will not leave us alone. Some of these hands indeed will try to do us a bit of good, shape us into a better pattern, help us to think straight, stretch our minds, open doors for us into larger kingdoms, introduce us to things that are true, beautiful and good. These are the people who love us and respect us and will stand by us through thick and thin. These are the grandfatherly and grandmotherly people, the fatherly and motherly people, the sisterly and brotherly people. They are the best.

But, on the other side, are the destroyers and the despoilers, the vandals and the wreckers. They'll try to pull you down to their own level, poison your mind, blight your hopes. They're everywhere.

The great thing is to decide that you will throw your weight and your fighting strength, on the side of the makers, and against the breakers. After all, you have one life to live, one mind to enlarge, one heart to guard, one soul to save. But I warn you fairly, the moral battle is long and hard and bitter, and often enough you will be mauled to the ground. The Apostle Paul found it so. He had no doubt about which side he was on, but, fight as he would, he was often brought down. Then he found the answer. And you heard it in the second lesson: "Take unto you the whole armour of God, helmet of salvation, shield of faith, sword of the Spirit," and so on. You may have thought, after all that rattle of steel, that it ends a little tamely—with all prayer, praying. But I have read that when the sleeping camp of the Roman formation was wakened by the blare of the alarm, the officers would be shouting: "Put on all armour," this was no scuffle but a deadly fight, *all* armour, and then when they were in tight battle array: "Now, then, lads, with all fighting strength, fighting." So Paul says: "With all prayer, praying," for when a Christian fights, he prays, and when he prays he fights. You see, when the Christian confronts this confused and tumbling life of much power and influence—some good and some bad, some making, some breaking—he calls in the clean strong powers of the invisible world. Yes, he calls in Christ.

THE PERFECT DETERGENT

1 John 1 : 7b : " . . . and the blood of Jesus Christ His Son cleanseth us from all sin."

NOT often have I walked with the mighty, but once on a day I walked with Will Sangster and tried to persuade him to write another book on preaching. He wanted to know what area he was to cover. I told him—the undisclosed secrets of the great preachers. He had himself the cinematographic gift; he preached in moving pictures. Let him discover the spell of others and tell us.

He never wrote the book. But I find for myself that feebly pursuing that search, a sort of geiger-counter develops in the brain. Is it the sound of the slow tearing of calico that I hear, or the faint trilling of a bell? No matter. I know that I am in the presence of something arresting which I must identify. So reading the First Epistle of John I was made to pause in the first dozen verses. I could see that when John was setting forth the forgiveness and remission of sins, he laid hold on words of uncommon strength, words like light, blood, cleanseth, all, faithful, righteous, liar, advocate, propitiation, the whole world. So doing, he reaches out and lays his hand on mighty, indisputable and irresistible doctrines, thus: " . . . faithful and righteous to forgive us our sins."

Faithful! Always this was the song of the saints and the cry of the prophets. He is faithful. They never tired of declaring it. This was their Rock. The earth might shake. The floods might sweep over them. The darkness might overwhelm them. But one thing was immovable. God was faithful.

And God was righteous. Echoing from the dim beginning of things was the cry of Abraham: "Shall not the Judge of all the earth do right?" And this was the unvarying theme of the prophets. It is hammered into heads of the sons of Jacob in the First of Isaiah: God will have righteousness. It became a title—"The Lord our Righteousness." None can forget the words of Amos: "Let justice roll down as waters, and righteousness as a mighty stream." Now see what John does. He guarantees the forgiveness of sins by the faithfulness and the justice of God. Deny forgiveness, and you deny the faithfulness and the righteousness. Perhaps we shall look deeper into this later on, but enough for now to see how John displays the forgiving mercy by showing it interwoven with two mighty and irresistible truths. Writing under the power of the Holy Spirit, he does not demur from taking words that have sinew and muscle and conjoining such words to ideas that pulse with power, as if he would muster all the strength he can and throw it into this declaration of forgiveness of sins. Holding that thought, it then occurs to us that we have known something of that buffeting force before. It's there in the Old Testament. What might be thought of as a certain extravagance of expression, a startling vividness of imagery. "Though your sins be as scarlet, they shall be as white as snow." "As far as the east is from the west, so far hath he removed our transgressions from us." "Thou wilt cast all their sins into the depth of the sea."

Now why? Why this summoning of force, this concentration of power? Why do we have a sense of a strong man putting forth his strength? Why? Because the thing to be done will need that strength, and the thing to be done is to

Pluck from the memory a rooted sorrow,
Raze out the written troubles of the brain
And with some sweet oblivious antidote
Cleanse the stuff'd bosom of that perilous stuff
Which weighs upon the heart.

But how may that be done? Can a thing done be as if it never were?

The Moving Finger writes; and, having writ,
Moves on: nor all thy Piety nor Wit
Shall lure it back to cancel half a Line,
Nor all thy Tears wash out a Word of it.

If forgiveness meant that the forensic penalty for sin is remitted, this would be high Gospel indeed, but what of the penalty that abides in the memory of the heinous thing done, the suppurating remorse, the spawning mischief that sinks deeper within and spreads further without?

"*Rooted* sorrow," says Macbeth, and we recoil with horror from the prospect of those poisonous fibres worming their ways deeper and deeper into the heart-soil. I find when I pluck up a weed, I lift with it its local habitation of soil. How could one possibly pluck from the memory a rooted sorrow?

It was early in my ministry that I beat against the granite wall. She was a woman approaching the middle years, respected and respectable. She had done a thing (she told me what) when she was twenty-one, and now the memory of it haunted her night and day. I suspected she was a melancholic (authors still used the expression in that day), but I applied the Gospel. I explained to her what the "unforgivable sin" was—she had used the expression, and then I took her to the great Scriptures, one after another. It seemed to avail nothing. I asked her to come with me there and then to the church where we would take the Lord's Supper together, the bread and wine the tokens of redemption wrought and free forgiveness. She would not come. She was past hope. She was in hospital for a considerable time. "Endogenous depression" they would call it today.

Outside the circle of what we normally think of as sickness, there are similar states of mind in the rich and varying experiences of religion. Jesus said that when the Holy Spirit came He would convince men of sin. The phrase "conviction of sin" is in common use. You find many instances in John Wesley's *Journal,* and more in every record of the movements of the Spirit. "In the course of the sermon, one of those present, John Stokes, cried out in great distress. He fell to the ground. He continued so while several of the brethren continued earnestly in prayer for the mercy of God. At four in the morning he found peace. Margaret Hallam, a woman of that place, was stricken, and had tears for her portion for ten days. Then God defeated Satan in her, and she knew her sins forgiven." Thus the *Journal.* I have been reading Owen Jones', *Some of the Great Preachers of Wales,* and find many more such instances. If it has not been done already, a work on the comparative study of conviction of sin and endogenous depression is overdue.

From there we move, strangely it may seem, to the deep experience of the saints. Alexander Whyte has been my guide here. Shepherd of Harvard, Andrew Bonar, Lancelot Andrewes, Jeremy Taylor, Fraser of Brea, Luther, Augustine. God lifted veil after veil from the plagued hearts of these men in the severity of His sanctifying work, but as each lifted veil showed more of the plague, redeeeming mercy showed more of the cleansing blood of Christ, yet more of His sweet grace. "Show me," cried Charles Wesley, "as my soul can bear the depth of inbred sin."

All this brings us with a large question to the great mass of mankind, ourselves included. We have our ups and downs, but we jog along with a fair amount of composure. We have a twinge of conscience now and then, a black mood from time to time, but otherwise a fairly even complacency. But who is nearer to reality—those with a sharp and piercing sense of sin, or those without it? *Gnothi seauton,* said the Greeks, "know thyself." Who best knows himself, the grieving saint or the complacent sinner?

The alienists of earlier days used to write long case-histories of those who came under their observation. The longest and most detailed account I know is by Morton Prince in his renowned work, *The Unconscious.* It concerns a respectable woman patient whom he treated over a span of years. She came to his notice through the Church Bells phobia which had gained no little currency. Later on she fell victim to depression. Careful following of the devious and backward track, he found at the root of her miseries the obscure working of a sense of shame. This is but one case. Read a hundred more and you will find the same malignant root.

Praise be that I do not have to explain to this instructed congregation why it is that this writhing horror can be at its deathly work night and day without being recognised by the sufferer. You know of repression and dissociation; the weaving of the veils that hide a man from himself.

You will not dispute it therefore when I say that most

of us are living in a fool's paradise, like a vine-grower on the slopes of Vesuvius, sipping his wine under his fig-tree of a summer evening while all hell boils beneath, or like this present world idly picking its teeth while it sits upon a stockpile of nuclear missiles. The phenomenon is not unknown. I remember a young fellow dying of consumption. Towards the end he became elated. He was sure he was getting better. They call it *spes phthisica,* "the consumptive's hope." You will come across cases of disseminated sclerosis where the patient is convinced he is fit and well, while everybody else knows he is getting worse. And that they call *eutonia sclerotica,* the well-being of the sclerotic. The French who have, perhaps, studied conversion hysteria (nothing to do with religion!) more than any other nation, have coined a phrase to hit off the bland and complacent disposition of a man suffering from, say, hysterical paralysis of both legs. They refer to *la belle indifference.*

Thus what I am saying is that there is a plague of the human heart whether it is known or unknown to its possessor. A man may be dead in trespasses and sins, but consciously feel and display a certain poise and ease of mind, at least when he is engrossed in his work or sport. It may be different in the small and sleepless hours. What both Scripture and psychology show is that this malaise is deep and spreading, and throwing off buds and malignant flowers which are poison and death. Heine had it that God would of course forgive sins, it was His trade, but we see it is no mere crossing out of a line in a book. The guilt is no mere record, like the figures in a ledger. A criminal once produced to me an official police form with a list of his convictions. Our guilt is not a mere list in God's black book. It is a real and living thing, alive with malignancy in man's being. As real as the bacillus of cholera, as the maverick cells of cancer. The thing has spread its clinging roots in the soul of every man, and its work is death, eternal death.

Thus, if it is to be dealt with, it must be plucked forth. In the language of our text it must be cleansed. You recall that queer little tale in Second Kings, chapter two, of how certain farmers complained to Elisha that the water was nought and the land miscarried. He required of them a new cruse containing salt. This he took to the source of the river and threw in the salt. The waters were healed. There was no more miscarrying.

A parable, is it not? of the human heart.

You who have so often been drawn into the hidden trouble of a family will know well enough how often sudden outbursts, strange aberrations, flaring tempers, dark moods in one or other of the family will set the rest on edge. In Morton Prince's patient, the writhing mischief underneath emerged first as a phobia, and then as a depression. But they only begin the list, the compulsive obsessions—to strike, to strangle, to kill—I speak of what I know, the unbalancing of the mind, the screaming lust, the murmuring spite, the corrupting envy, the mad ambition. Is there an end to it? O, for the magic salt that could cleanse the first and last and every bubbling spring of the human heart!

I turn again to First John and his opening chapter. At one of Campbell Morgan's evangelistic meetings in Canada, they found in the collection plate a written note pinned to a bank-note. The written note said something to the effect that the money was for the preaching of the Gospel from one who was beyond it.

Now I dare something with my imagination that I may be instructed myself, and offer instruction to you.

I see the Apostle John catching up with that man as

he leaves that place and goes down his dark road to his dark house. John goes with superb confidence, for some-one goes with him, not to be seen, but John knows that He holds a chalice in His nail-pierced hands, and the chalice is brimming with the mystic blood of Christ. He falls in step with His new companion, and after words of introduction, tells him He knows the plague of his heart, and that He has a healing medicine for it: "If we walk in the light, as He is in the light, we have fellow-ship one with another, and the blood of Jesus Christ, His Son, cleanseth us from all sin." And John sees the vivid image again, all the channels, and drains, and run-nels in the depths of the man's soul, and all the pits and crevices and crannies in the man's soul, all the stench and the miasma, all the guilt and shame, here caked and hard, here bubbling and suppurating, and all with a clinging adhesive power. But John has seen what the blood of Christ can do. It cleanses, down every channel, down every drain, it swirls, seeks out the cross-channels and the pockets, the old caked guilt, and the new bubbling shame. It scours, scrubs, cleanses. How many times has John seen the effect of its power! Men changed, men laughing, men crying for joy, men dancing in their walk, men singing their heads off! And now he thinks it will have power with this man who left the note in the collection plate. But the man holds him off. "It is kind of you to speak, and I know it works for some, but d'you see, I do not walk in the light, deep and dark has been my fall. Even the midday light is pain to me, for it makes my darkness the darker. The springtime is a distress to me; I say:

How can ye chaunt, ye little birds,
And I'm sae weary, fu' o' care.

Nay, we do not have fellowship one with the other, for you are in the light and I am in the dark. Let me be."

"But," says John, "one thing is clear to me, you know your sins and you have confessed your sin. Hear this: 'If we confess our sins, He is faithful and just to forgive us our sins, and to cleanse us from all unrighteousness.'" "Faithful," mark that! Will you now stand in the face of all Scripture, and in the face of millions who swear by the faithfulness of God, will you now look into the face of Jesus Christ, and declare that God is unfaithful? Something more, if there is one thing that all the seers and the prophets, and all the saints and visionaries have hammered into our heads, it is that God is just. Will you now stand there and shout out to everybody that God is not righteous? Well, then: "He is faithful and just to forgive us our sins, and to cleanse us from all unrighteousness."

"Nay but," says that so tormented man, "my head cannot answer your argument, but the last spark of faith is snuffed out in my heart. I hear what you say, but I cannot rise to it. Put forgiveness into my hand and close my fingers over it—I could not hold it. The pith has gone out of my fingers. Let me go now."

"But," says John, "if I were to let you go, there is One who will not let you go. Have you not heard that if any man sin we have an Advocate with the Father, Jesus Christ the Righteous. You mind how there at Calvary, when they threw Him down on the wooden frame, and began to drive the spikes into His hands and feet, He commenced to pray: 'Father, forgive them, for they know not what they do,'" and went on repeating that prayer. Counsel for the defence was He, pleading for the hate-filled men who did this thing. And do you not know that now, while I speak, He pleads for you before the Throne in the Heavenly Place, pleads for you by name, and every time He speaks your name He caresses it with love, your name being written on His hands?"

"My name?" says the other, "My name! But no, it cannot be. My name is worthless. Yet, as you have spoken, something has briefly come and gone again. What? A gleam of light? Like the hint of the dawn, but the night has come again."

"Now hear me," says John. "He is the propitiation for our sins, and not for ours only, but for the sins of the whole world. You have tried to make some propitiation for your sin. That ten-pound note in the collection. Other things too. So sin-ridden men did in the old days. Lambs and goats and bulls they brought until the altar gutters were awash with blood. Some used to flog themselves. Lived high and lonely on pillars of stone. Put down silver and gold for pardons. Left land to the Church. Propitiation, always propitiation! As deep as our nature goes we have a sense that sins cannot be smudged away by mere word. The awful sin needs an awful propitiation. And it was made! It was made by God's Son, lately come from the glory of the Eternal Palaces for this very purpose, arriving at the appointed place, Calvary; and arriving at the appointed time for the flogging, the blows, the crown of thorns and the nails, and the dying crimson like a robe flowing o'er His body on the Tree. No man has touched more than the fringe of Christ's robe of suffering, for He was making propitiation for our sins, and not for ours only, but for the sins of the whole world. Man, d'you hear that? The sins of the whole world! And if for the sins of the whole world, then for yours, just as for mine."

The other halted. "What's happening?" he said. "I'm away in a little hut on the edge of the prairie years ago. My father and mother are there. I must have been little. We left that place when I was five. But I can hear them singing; how does it go?

And the burden of my heart rolled away,
And the burden of my heart rolled away.

And it has taken me all this time to know what they meant. My dear, God-given friend, the burden of my heart has rolled away."

If I were speaking now to a company of politicians, I should be piercingly aware of how the land miscarries, and of how daunting is their task by this device and that, by rule and regulation, to mitigate the evil. But they do not have this mystic and potent salt to cleanse the place of the springing waters.

So if I were speaking to a company of psychiatrists. These men come closer. Their work is at the springing of the waters, "for out of the heart are the issues of life." Never under-reckon their prodigious labours, or their dedication, or their intelligence; but, as Kalinowski says: "We are treating disorders the origin of which we do not know, by methods which are shrouded in mystery." Psychiatrists, *qua* psychiatrists, do not have the salt either.

But I speak to a company who have been called, appointed and ordained to carrying the healing medicines of God to the human heart; so to believe, so to pray, so to preach that the cleansing blood of Christ may wash clean the human heart.

God make us sufficient for these things!

SURE HARVEST

1 Cor. 15:58: Wherefore, my beloved brethren, be ye steadfast unmoveable, always abounding in the work of the Lord, forasmuch as ye know that your labour is not vain in the Lord.

IN the year 1835, Thomas Carlyle, essayist and historian, had completed the first volume, itself an enormous work, the first volume of his perhaps most notable work, *The French Revolution.* He lent this massive manuscript to his friend, John Stuart Mill. Mill's servant girl found a pile of paper early one morning, and thinking it was rubbish, put it on the fire.

Carlyle reeled under the blow, but set to at once to write it again . . . But what a blow . . . Months of pen-scratching, setting down the fruit of careful research . . . the annotating, the choosing of words, the balancing of sentences . . . and now gone in a puff of smoke . . .

That kind of experience of course in many different forms, and of course with different intensities, can happen to many. Times of recession multiply the number. A man by dint of hard work and enterprise can build a business, have the satisfaction of seeing it expand, be assured that his son or sons can take over in due time . . . but then the market begins to shrivel, raw materials come to fantastic prices . . . overseas competition . . . and so on, and so on. And then on-a-day, the factory doors are closed . . . It's hard to see the labour of the years go for nothing . . .

But in every field . . . the sculptor with an unready stroke ruins the masterpiece under his hands . . . the struggling artist dreams of recognition . . . but his pictures are never hung . . . The research doctor is on the track of a cure, goes on with mounting hope, but finally, put to the test, he knows that the years and the labour have gone for nothing. And the taste of gall is on the tongue . . .

Peculiarly prone to this bitter melancholy are those who traffic in the invisible . . . Those whose commerce is in ideas, in the hope that they will fructify in the minds of others. But ideas and minds are both invisible. The men who are called upon to persuade, persuade to better things, persuade to faith, persuade to hope . . . but the force and cogency of persuasion are both invisible, and we can never see them enter the portals of the mind, never see them.

Pondering all this, you will see at once why it is that the usefulness of spiritual labour is impossible to assess. Its commerce and traffic is between mind and mind, and between heart and heart, and there is always a veil over the secret mind, and there is always a cloak over the hidden heart. A preacher breaks out the Word of God, and there is a ferment of forces in the deep places of the soul . . . but they are unseen . . . A teacher in the Sunday school takes his class through their lesson, and the pressure of thoughts and ideas are at work in the heads of the children . . . but no eye can see it. Indeed the witness is often not by word, but by deed, no word may be spoken at all. Watchful eyes see the bearing of a Christian man in his day of trouble . . . but both witness and watcher go each his way, and nothing is ever said.

There is no tape-measure for all this. No balance to weigh the matter.

The woodworker can polish the table he has fashioned; the home-dressmaker can hold up the frock she has made; but the Christian worker deals for the most part in invisibles.

And yet from time to time, a *glimpse* is given here and there almost as if, by *divine providence* . . . something is plucked from the invisible and given a body. As if God says: "It is time this thirsty pilgrim of Mine is given some refreshment on the road . . . "

So long ago I stood on Crewe Station and Will Sangster, deeply revered, almost cannoned into me. It appeared that he and I were both for the Liverpool train. Now he had a most embarrasing trick of calling for the advice of lesser men, and there in the crowded compartment he outlined his problem, his problem and that of a multitude more. The problem of the fruit for our labour . . . much sowing but a meagre harvest . . . a torrent of words but little reply. "I preach at Westminster every Sunday, and then I am at meetings up and down the country" . . . he said, "I conduct fellowships and weekend conferences. I preach in the open air . . . I write . . . I write newspaper articles, pamphlets . . . books, perhaps of some weight, and books in between. . . but where is it all getting us? I, daunted at the demand to say something he hadn't already thought of, was suddenly undaunted. You wrote a book . . . *He is able."* He looked apologetic. "Well," said I, "I read this book of yours for the second time this last week, and when I had finished it I went into the Church of England chaplain's office next door . . . a fellow called Spurgin. I chucked your book on his table and said: 'Read that, Spurgin, it'll do your soul good.' 'Well,' I said, 'there was silence next for the space of about two hours . . . and then Spurgin came in flourishing your book, 'Mac,' he said, 'this is mighty, I shall preach from this on Sunday.' 'So,' I said, 'the message of your book will be preached to about a thousand men in the hangar next Sunday morning.'" He put his hands together and lifted his face . . . and said: *"Praise God."* I think perhaps the Eternal Spirit was saying to him . . . : "Will Sangster, Be ye steadfast, unmoveable . . . your labour is not in vain in the Lord . . . "

So motoring on a road well to the west your eye will be drawn to a dip between the hills and perhaps the dip is thick with trees, but none the less you catch a glimpse, only a glimpse, of the blue sea . . . You drive on . . . but you never think that glimpse is all the sea there is . . . Nay, you know that it stretches to the far horizon, and well beyond the vastness engirdling the world.

So from time to time we have a glimpse, only a glimpse, of the tides and currents of the world invisible . . . but we know it is only a glimpse . . . there in the length and breadth of the spiritual universe, and in the unfathomable depths . . . the forces of spiritual power move and deploy . . . and the labour is not vain in the Lord.

Late arrival or Time lag

Next I draw your attention to the phenomenon of the late arrival. One obvious example derives from the immensity of the universe. Every schoolboy knows that light takes time to travel . . . He knows its speed . . . 186,000 miles a second. Thus he knows that the light by which he now reads his book, started from the sun eight minutes or so before. But this is nothing. There are far-off lights that blaze in the eye of the telescope that began their far journey millions of years ago. Late arrivals indeed.

You know that mammoths have been found in Siberia, deep frozen with uncorrupted food still in the mouth. Russian scientists have a startling project . . . to animate the unfrozen tissue, and by various processes to take the genes and chromosomes and from them, produce a clone . . . a living mammoth. If ever they do that, it will indeed be a late arrival.

In a different way, a desert will sometimes welcome a late arrival. Some freak storm will soak the sands that have not known rain for ages . . . And then soon after there is a carpet of flowers in that place. When was it that those seeds fell from their parent flowers? Were they carried there by the wind, and by the wind covered in the sterile sand? But when? Late arrivals indeed, born long after their due time.

There is a parallel in the world of ideas. One can scarcely read a book of high philosophy without contemplating the thought of Plato who lived four hundred years before Christ, and of Aristotle who followed hard on Plato. It is not simply that these ideas come cocooned in the web of the centuries, but they come to fructify in the minds of modern men, displaying new facets of truth, new gleams of light. But, that apart, here in the Church of God, modern men drive shafts into the rich mines of Holy Scripture, and often enough people will say, "I never saw that before," and God has yet more light to break out of His holy Word.

And, after that each man has his own late arrivals . . . For in the journey from birth to the grave, each man is storing up the vast treasures of his experience. Memory is a strange thing. Some things are readily recalled and yesterday becomes today . . . But there is clear evidence that lying deeper than these ready memories, there is stored up an immense resource of experiences and that they are charged with power, some for good and some for ill, obscurely shaping the pattern of his life, obscurely directing his daily behaviour.

Years ago I attended a meeting addressed by Dr. Bhusia, one of the great African and Christian leaders of that day. Near to me sat a retired missionary. It was in that missionary's home that Dr. Bhusia was a houseboy. In that home he saw the daily pattern of Christian living, and in that home he heard of the Saviour . . . I suppose that in that missionary's heart the Spirit was whispering: "Your labour is not vain in the Lord."

There is nothing particularly solemn in the way the children stream out of Sunday School, but if we could see all and know all, and if the future was written for us to read, each one of us would be weighed down with an awful solemnity . . . What shaping is taking place, what directions of course are being settled . . . what emergency help is being laid up! What grace stored for future days!

Once, having visited one of my church officers in hospital, I was making my way out of the ward when a patient raised a finger to me. I went over. Without preliminary, he said: "What's that bit about the saddle and the ground . . . ?" "I think, strictly, the quotation is about the *stirrup* and the ground," I said: "Betwixt the saddle and the ground, I mercy sought and mercy found." "Yes," he said, "that's it. Is it true?" I said "What's the matter?" He told me he'd been brought in a few days before. It was his heart. He guessed it was pretty well shot at. He thought he might be going out of there in a box. That was why he wanted to know about the saddle and the ground. He said he'd never bothered us fellows much. In fact he hadn't been to church since he left Sunday School, but it was in Sunday School that he'd heard about the saddle and the ground. Is it true? "O, it's true, all right," I said, "and if you turn to God now He will receive you. D'you want to?" He nodded. So we prayed. I had a postcard a few days later telling me he'd slept that night in the peace of God.

That's what I mean by late arrival. Some Sunday School teacher in those far-off days, trying to cope with a squad of restless boys, thinking sometimes that it was like talking to a brick wall . . . thinking time and again that he ought to resign. But one day he quoted the bit about the saddle and the ground, and years and years later it was the savour of life to a dying man.

But it is probable that he never knew, never knew until he arrived in the better country. I do not know how they manage things there, but maybe a special messenger told him of this thing, and then the angel would say, "I am instructed to say, that your labour was not vain in the Lord."

But now finally, see where this heartening Scripture comes . . . It comes to clinch the high doctrine of one of the mightiest chapters in the Book . . . The prophetic vision sweeps us on to the consummation of all things . . . to the day when the trumpet shall sound, and the heavens are ablaze with light. To the day of the great change . . . And we shall be changed . . . to that day all things move, for God is working His purpose out, and we who are fellow-workers with God are working His purpose out . . . and in that day all Christian work will be fulfilled and crowned.

The work of our fathers, whether they preached or taught or witnessed, whether they laboured to lift their fellow-men, whether they set one stone on another to build a house for God, whether they gave of their substance to send others overseas, whether they dusted the pews, or brought flowers for the Lord's Table . . . all that work will be fulfilled and crowned on the day when history is rolled like a scroll. And that of myriads of Christian people in every place, saints, apostles, martyrs . . . those who dared the stake, those who suffered or died behind prison bars . . .

All that will be fulfilled and crowned on that day when the trumpet shall sound and the dead shall be raised incorruptible and we shall be changed.

Your labour is not vain in the Lord, for all your labour moves and tends toward that day. You may see little fruit for it here and now, but then and there it will receive its glittering crown . . . for the greatness and the wonder of that majestic day will be in part compounded by the work you do now . . .

What a consummation that will be! For "this corruptible must put on incorruption" . . . How we feel this corruptible . . . Physiology tells us of it . . . psychology tells us of it . . . but we do not need these erudite teachers . . . we know it in our bones . . . soon after our youth we grimly recognise our diminishing powers . . . The Olympic swimmers seem to fade off after twenty . . . The boxing ring reads a lesson to the erstwhile champion, reads the lesson of this corruptible . . . As to the mind, we hear ruefully that intelligence tends to diminish after 18 years, though we still hope to gain wisdom . . . And then as the years pass, the signals of this corruptible come thick and fast . . . and the grim and undeniable fact is that we live in a dying body . . . But this corruptible must put on incorruption . . . must . . . hear that? What a change that will be! I wonder how long it will take for us to get used to our new clothes . . . when this corruptible has put on incorruption!

And this mortal must put on immortality . . . Imagine that! Here and now the dark shape of mortality is always at the shoulder. It's not that we are always thinking of it in a deliberate way, but that shadow is always there. We notice it the more when a young child is mysteriously sick or when children, out on their bikes, are late. Or when there's a greyness on the faces of the old folk, or when the autumn leaves are falling, or when there is a melancholy in the air.

But this mortal shall put on immortality. What is it like when that shadow is gone? What is it like when you know the springing waters of the well of life will never cease?

"Then shall be brought to pass the saying that is written, Death is swallowed up in victory . . . "

Then "Thanks be to God which giveth us the victory through our Lord Jesus Christ."

See, then, the rapture that sweeps the mind of the apostle. Whatever the immediate ends for which we work for Christ, they are all gathered up in that triumphant end when the trumpet shall sound, and we shall be changed.

"Wherefore, my beloved brethren, be ye steadfast, unmovable, always abounding in the work of the Lord forasmuch as ye know that your labour is not vain in the Lord."

WORKING WORKMANSHIP

Ephesians, 2, 10: For we are His workmanship, created in Christ Jesus unto good works.

THAT TOUCHES A deep chord. It must be the trace of our original creation. We were made in the image of God. He delights to make things. So do we. The creative urge is tight-bound in that bundle of mysteries that makes our human nature. So important is it that, if a man makes nothing, something will turn sour within him. When a man breaks down, it is of first importance to put his hands to work. In the hospitals concerned, they have their occupational therapy, and some have industrial units. Creativeness at work is a healing medicine.

The field of creation seems to be illimitably wide. Winston Churchill had a flair for painting pictures and building walls. Principal Chaplain Stanley Keen liked building walls. So do I. The satisfaction is indefinable. What is yours? Knitting, gardening, carpentry, marquetry, painting, papering walls, model-making? We may begin the list; we can never end it.

We find a sanctity upon these things when our minds go back to the workshop high on the hill at Nazareth, and have a curious sense of earthly fellowship with the divine when we smell the tang of freshly cut wood, and see the feet of our blessed Lord in the shavings on the floor, see His measuring eye upon the work, the ripple of the muscles as He planes or chisels.

And then our thoughts out-soar the stars as we consider the great Creator, our Heavenly Father, for He also is a Workman. But it is too much, altogether too much, even to glance at the pageant of creation that is His. Why, one single sunset can at times quite overcome the spirit; but what of the splendours of the setting of ten million, million suns spread throughout the unnumbered galaxies, unseen by any created eye . . . except perhaps by the eyes of angels? With something like relief we drop our gaze to this hither-world.

But our wonder and our praise are not abated. Splendour and magnificence still we see, but with it a gentler beauty of hill and valley, and the shy loveliness of the flowers. And then with microscope we catch and hold our breath at the perfection of the incredibly small.

For these things Scripture has a glance and more than a glance, and breaks out in eloquent praise. But the burden of Scripture concerns that creativeness for which God Almighty puts forth His strength and skill and Divine determination. The creativeness which goes forth to handle, to shape and to mould the rough and broken stuff of our human nature. As if all the rest of creation might have been wrought by a twirl of the finger of omnipotence . . . but for this other, the unflagging patience of the centuries, the pain that must be endured, the price that must be paid down. We are His workmanship. We are to be His masterpiece. The Scripture sees Him draw near with infinite graciousness to some marred and disfigured creature, rotten with the inherited taint of a thousand generations, ugly with the ultimate ugliness of sin, a creature that fiercely spurns the touch of those moulding, shaping fingers — which one of us has not struck away the hand of God, pulled our rags about us, and fled into our stinking lair? But the Divine Workman is patient with the patience of infinite love; and still He draws near, and some men can tell how He waited and pleaded and pleaded and waited from their boyhood to old age. But with this one and that the moment of surrender, and the work begins. But what material this is! Surely only God would take this work in hand. What strong and ancient sins run their disfigurement through the piece! Take them out, one would think, and the stuff will fall to pieces! With sculptor or painter the materials and instruments are inanimate. But God's material is living flesh and soul; sometimes it is docile, sometimes rebellious; now it submits to the Master's hand, now it struggles to escape. "Fill Thou my life," so it sings on a Sunday night, and on a Wednesday morning snarls out, "Leave me alone!" But the Divine patience never wearies. And so perhaps something is done. There is a gleam of beauty, a change appearing over the years. And then a desperate moment, with the black blood in our brain, we smash the thing to pieces.

And then? Then He begins again.

And what does He mean to make out of this marred and disfigured creature? Any improvement at all would be a triumph. If He could supplant some of the ugliness with something of beauty . . . If He could offset the broken and jagged angles with some gracious line . . .

Now will you hear it? Hearing, will you lay hold on it? Will you keep your grip on it, though it seems against all possibility? We are foreordained to be conformed to the image of His Son. We shall be like Him, for we shall see Him as He is.

If you've ever been at one of those question-and-answer open-air meetings, the soap-box kind of thing, you will know how the questions come thick and fast. And if it is a regular thing, the regulars will be waiting for you. And some of them know their Bibles well, and they know all the awkward questions to ask. It always seemed to me odd that no one ever read out that passage about being conformed to the image of His Son, and then asked if I really believed that one day I should be like Jesus Christ. Like the hymn-writer,

I cannot look upon His face
For shame, for bitter shame.

And yet the promise is there. "He that began a good work in you will perfect it unto the day of Jesus Christ." "We are foreordainded to be conformed to the image of His Son." "We shall be like Him, for we shall see Him as He is." And though this tugs at the anchors of my belief; and though the vision of it is blurred and dim, I see it must be so. He is God, and the Divine Artist can never rest this side of perfection. Working once with my brother on a thing of wood, I, all impatience, said, "There, that's fine!" He looked at me with astonishment and rebuke. "It's a sixteenth of an inch out," he said, and plied his tool again. Massillon, the renowned French preacher, would sometimes write out his sermon twenty times. The backward trail of humanity is littered with the spill-over from waste-paper baskets, poems crumpled up, pages torn across, canvasses ripped down, sculpture hammered to fragments, for when the true creative urge is upon a man he has a dream, and that dream is perfection. Shall God be less than that? Shall God ever say, "There, that will do?" Nay, but as He works, He has ever before Him the image of His Son, and this that He does must be conformed to that image. We are His workmanship.

Now the text goes on: " . . . created in Christ Jesus unto good works."

If we turn to 1 Corinthians 3, 9, we read that we are "labourers together with God," or that we are God's fellow-workers. Here is a startling conjunction of ideas! The thing being created is to be a creator. The workmanship is to work. Turning to Corinthians 3 again, we read that we are God's husbandry; it means we are God's ploughed field. We know that we are the sheep of His pasture, the ambassadors of God, the letters of Christ, but God's ploughed field! Yes, but, do you see, we are the labourers sent into the harvest. We are men to be fished for, and then fishers of men. We are sheep, and then we are the under-shepherds of the flock. We are His workmanship, and while still his workmanship, we are fellow-workers with God. A paradox indeed, but what vistas it opens up!

Small-seeming things it may be. "Consider the ravens," said Jesus, "God feedeth them." And when the snow is thick, and the birds are hungry, and you sweep clean your bird-table, and load it with scraps and crumbs, you are entitled to say to yourself, "Fellow-worker with God." And you read how it says, " . . . the desert shall rejoice and blossom as the rose," " . . . and in the wilderness shall waters break out, and streams in the desert." Once North Africa was the granary of the Roman Empire, but the sands swept over it. Now attempts are being made by irrigation and afforestation to make it a fruitful land again. Keep at it, ye fellow-workers with God.

And then after that, the great running sores of the world, the wounds that fester without hope of cure, the plagues that rage without abatement, the children that cry for bread, and crying, die. But over against it, the ships that sail loaded with grain, the aircraft loaded with medical supplies, the bales of clothing, parcels made up, teams of workers, hives of collectors, regiments of open-handed givers. Do you doubt it? Fellow-workers with God.

"Created in Christ Jesus unto good works," says the text, and we are here a strand of the broad redeeming strategy of God Almighty. The redeemed are to be the agents of redemption. The man saved by the Word becomes a servant of the Word. It is the Divine multiplication. You see it neatly and simply in the preaching mission. A man is called into salvation; subsequently he is called to preach. Under his preaching many are called to salvation, and among that company some who are called to preach. Now each of those in his turn . . . but what need to go on?

When He first the work began,
Small and feeble was its day.
Now the Word doth switly run,
Now it wins its widening way.

More and more it spreads and grows,
Ever mighty to prevail;
Sin's stronghold it now o'erthrows,
Shakes the trembling gates of hell.

But we are to see not only the broad strategy in time and eternity, we are to see this creation unto good works as particular and peculiar and vital to this man, this piece of living workmanship with which the fingers of God are busy, for if there be no issuing forth of good works, the work is in abeyance; it is impeded; if I may so put it, the fingers of God are still.

I think it was F. B. Meyer who pointed out the significance of the difference between the Sea of Galilee and the Dead Sea. Both lie in the same rift, both are fed by the River Jordan. The Sea of Galilee is alive, fish swim in its waters; birds nest on its banks; the gardens, and the orchards and the vineyards flourish there. But the Dead Sea is dead — no fish, no birds, no fruit. The reason is the while the Jordan flows into Galilee, it also flows out. But nothing flows out of the Dead Sea. Which things are a parable. The religious-seeming life out of which nothing flows is dead. I do not mean that an outflowing of good works is a symptom of the developing spiritual life, it is the burgeoning of the spiritual life itself.

Now let us go on to the clinching truth. We have seen that the workmanship of God is many-faceted. His creativeness moves over a vast field, but when the purpose of God is centred most intensively — I speak after the manner of men — when His eye is fixed unwaveringly, when His strength and skill and delicacy are vested most in His shaping and moulding fingers, when He is ready for the utmost price, when He will spare nothing — not even His only-begotten Son — it is when He is intent to bring many sons unto glory, then He is employed in conforming this rough, broken, tainted human stuff into the image of His Son. And see what follows, though to see it staggers the mind, when we are appointed as fellow-workers with Him, we are called to the same business, the same trade.

This is our high calling. There is many a noble calling in this life. I have always thought that that of the schoolteacher was a noble calling. To have a part in shaping the destiny of these, so young, so impressionable, so malleable. To open doors for them into the wide world of knowledge. To implant ideals of industry and honour and service. Difficult, yes. Too often the tides and currents are running the other way. But it's a bonny battle to fight, and something of abiding worth will lodge in those young minds, and abide through life.

That of a doctor is a noble calling. A high privilege it is to be called into a house where the breadwinner is laid low, and to take charge, and to fight back the mysterious illness, and beat back the fears, and then, later, to know that recovery is on its way, and perhaps two months on to pass down that street in your car, and see the man coming home from work, and a child hanging on the garden-gate chattering a welcome. Mighty!

But what higher calling can there be than to be fellow-workers with God? A man I heard of was on holiday in the south country. He had, like many more, an interest in old parish churches. Then he heard that a new one was being built in his holiday locality. He went to see it, and found the architect on the site. The architect, recognising an enthusiast, took him into the site office and showed him the plans. The visitor stared and wondered. The mass of detail was astonishing. Even the places where the nails were to be driven in were marked. the architect said, "We are not building just for the first thousand years, you know."

And God's workmanship is not just for the first thousand years, but for eternity, and those who are fellow-workers with God are not building just for the first thousand years, but for eternity. There is a city whose Maker and Builder is God, and already we are who in Christ are the citizens of that New Jerusalem. And now, while we tarry amid the decaying dust of the cities of this world, our business, in partnership with God, is the creation of that eternal citizenry.

Some who hear this will have a love for their gardens. On holiday, a quiet amble through some famous garden will be their pleasure. On a winter's night, they will con the seed and bulb catalogues. On a spring day, they will be out in their patch, and cherish each hour they can spare during summer nights. You then, who can do such things, do you not know that there is many a life without a gleam of colour in it? Many a life infested with weeds? Could you do something about that? You know that a flicker of hope can be the beginning of new life, and that hope runs close with faith. You will remember how the Lord Jesus, facing some disaster of a life, would strive for some spark of faith. Can you do that? How? Nay, don't ask me. You have a partner. Ask Him.

Or you fancy yourself as a Do-It-Yourself man. You love tools, and you love a bit of a challenge. Ay, times have been when a piece of furniture has succumbed, or a tearful child has presented you with the broken pieces of a toy, and you have dragged out the box of tools, looked for a bit of wood, or a bit of metal, whistled as you worked, filed, sand-papered, given something a lick of paint perhaps. Ah, me! it touches something deep when you mend a broken thing.

Could you make shift to mend a broken life? Well, that's something else. Yes, indeed. But that is God's trade. There He so often begins in the ongoing of making what is to be a thing of beauty and a joy for ever. Listen! He is calling: "Hey! fellow-worker, lend a hand."

"For we are his workmanship, created in Christ Jesus unto good works."